Come Hon

Long Lost Lore of Cooking Traditions in 19th Century Kentucky

Come Home, It's Suppertime

Long Lost Lore of Cooking Traditions in 19th Century Kentucky

By

LaVerne Martin Littleton

Bookstand Publishing

www.bookstandpublishing.com

Published by
Bookstand Publishing
Morgan Hill, CA 95037
3651_1

Copyright © 2011 by LaVerne Martin Littleton
All rights reserved. No part of this publication may be reproduced or transmitted in any form or by any means, electronic or mechanical, including photocopy, recording, or any information storage and retrieval system, without permission in writing from the copyright owner.

ISBN 978-1-61863-290-6

Printed in the United States of America

This book is dedicated
to

My beautiful Mother
Ada Elizabeth Peak Martin

Children
Danette and Robyn

Granddaughter
Beth

Great-Grandchildren
Gabriela, Nikolas, and Oliver

The book title comes from childhood memories when Mama called us in from playing. Even now, I can hear her voice calling me...

Come home... It's suppertime

I am thankful for her wisdom, patience, generosity, and grace.

My Sweet Home - Kentucky

Statehood - June 1, 1792
Capital City - Frankfort
State Tree - Tulip Poplar
State Flower - Goldenrod
State Bird - Cardinal

Notable People from My Home Town, Paducah

Irvin S. Cobb
Author, Humorist, and Character of Note
Gave advice on how to make the perfect Mint Julep
Who has not tasted one of mine has lived in vain.

Alben W. Barkley
US Representative from Kentucky
US Senator from Kentucky
35th Vice-President, 1949-1953, Harry S. Truman, President

In 1956, the Veep as he was affectionately called, died of a heart attack while giving a speech at Washington and Lee University in Virginia. Moments before he collapsed he said, *I am glad to sit on the back row now, for I would rather be a servant in the House of the Lord than to sit in the seats of the mighty.*

CONTENTS

Introduction	ix
My Story	1
My Mother	12
Bumblebee Cotton	14
Growing Up	19
My Town	24
Then and Now	27
I Remember...	
Cooking Secrets	31
Mama's Healing Remedies and Treatments for Sickness	33
When People Were Thrifty	35
Firsts	36

RECIPES

Kentucky – 1800's	37
Beverages	37
Soups	39
Vegetables	39
Desserts	42
Breakfast	45
Soups & Appetizers	55
Appetizers	59
Salads, Dressings, & Sauces	63
Vegetables	79
Entrees	91

Seafood	111
Breads	115
Pies	121
Cakes, Icings & Frostings	143
Candy & Cookies	165
Beverages	177

INTRODUCTION

When I started putting together a collection of old and new recipes for my children, it brought back many memories of times, places, foods, and stories of growing up with my family, friends, and neighbors. With each recipe, I made notes until the present book came about.

My parents were from original settlers in Kentucky. *We The People* have a long line of great cooks. However, not many recipes were written down - just passed by word-of-mouth from mother to daughter. By the early 1700's, women in France were said to be the first to write ingredients in order for their recipes. In one found copy, it seemed the cook taught her children music while preparing meals or planning them. Her recipes were written in the back of her children's music books.

In her kitchen, my Grandmother had a big barrel of flour. As a child, I would look in to see if the flour was getting low and she needed more. Grandmother always had fresh cakes and a pie or two in the pie safe. She calculated measurements for her ingredients by size of an egg or walnut and a pinch of this or that. My mother never owned a cookbook or measuring cups or spoons, either. She used Grandmother's ways and the palm of her hand for measuring salt, baking power. She used food scales to measure by the pound, butter, sugar, flour, and dried fruits. All their dishes and desserts turned out perfect and delicious. Mama had a round china cup with the handle broken off she used to measure liquids. It came out of a set of dishes from her early-married life. I wish I had them today for the sweet memories of Mama and me in her kitchen. She checked the wood stove oven temperature with her hand. If it felt too hot, she'd move one of the stove caps to cool the oven down. She'd check it again and if necessary, put the cap in place again. Daily, she baked cakes, pies, and bread with only her sensitivity to time and temperature. Her biscuits were light as a feather... Like Grandma, her cooking was superb without the conveniences of electronic appliances.

Food and love go hand-in-hand. From these childhood memories, It is my hope to pass down to my great-grand children and their children love and respect for daily life and bread.

Do not grasp at the stars, but do life's plain common work as it comes, certain that daily duties and daily bread are the sweetest things in life.

Robert Louis Stevenson

MY STORY

Author LaVerne Littleton's Parents: Ada Elizabeth Peak Martin, 1883–1968 and Lynn Ervine Martin, 1880–1967

I grew up in a small town in Western Kentucky along the banks of the Ohio and Tennessee rivers with my parents, Ada and Lynn, three brothers and two sisters. When I was a year old, my family left our McCracken County farm and moved into town. We lost the farm due to a bad business deal. Dad was a farmer, not a businessman. He bought the property, on a handshake, with a local physician. However, when the Illinois Central Railroad Company wanted to purchase the land across the back of our property, the doctor made a deal with ICRR to sell the farm and refused to share the profits. My parents managed to hang on until shortly before the stock market crash in 1929. The Great Depression left many broken hearts and families, like ours.

People worked hard and shared what they had with others who had less. Family and friends tried to keep up with special events such as weddings, holidays, picnics and births and deaths. We put on our best dresses and brought dishes of food prepared for whatever the event. I will always treasure Mr. Red's sorghum taffy pulls. He was a river captain working the Ohio, Tennessee, and Mississippi rivers. When he was home, he called all the children on our block for his famous taffy pulls. In the kitchen, he had a big candy hook on the wall where he'd throw and pull, throw and pull the taffy. He'd let us kids add the red or green coloring just before time to put the candy on a big marble slab (taffy won't stick to cold marble). Mr. Red would shape it in rolls or squares and slice it. Mr. Red and his wife didn't have children of their own; they loved all of us.

    I remember life back then when friends and neighbors really cared about each other's needs - whatever the need. I loved my street. I knew all my neighbors. Mama was known for her knowledge of folk medicine. She treated the sick and helped deliver babies. We took food to the sick or the down-and-out, as we called it. Many could not afford medicine or doctors. Mama took care of Aunt Clara whom I loved dearly. I didn't learn until I was older, that she was not really my aunt. Aunt Clara was born a slave. Her family lived and worked a farm just outside town. She was a very small child during the Civil War when General Ulysses S. Grant and the Union army took possession of our town to control the mouth of the Ohio and Tennessee Rivers. Aunt Clara recalled a horrifying event when the soldiers approached their farmhouse that day. Cooking in the back yard was a big, black iron kettle of boiling pumpkin, stirred by a little girl. Without reason or warning, one of the soldiers threw Clara into the scalding, thick pumpkin. Her legs were severely burned. Injuries she suffered from all her life. After her family had all passed away, she moved in town to a little house behind ours. I loved being with her. She was a great cook and I ate many meals with her. She worked in a restaurant from early morning until after lunch for many years until her legs became more and more painful and swollen. Finally, she had to quit her job. By then the skin on her legs began to break open and she developed a serious infection. Mama called the Health Department because she knew Aunt

Clara's condition was life threatening. The doctor prescribed live maggots to clean out the infection and heal the wounds. To treat Aunt Clara, the doctor and a nurse brought in twelve male larvae. Each day, they came to check on her treatment. Mama took care of her until her legs healed. I don't remember how long it took, but I remember she was in great pain. I was happy when she was well again. I loved her so. She passed away a year or so later. She lived more than 100 years of goodness and grace.

When a loved one passed, friends may have learned about it at the clothesline – it was the morning news - who was sick or lost a job, news of a wedding or new baby - traveled from yard to yard, line by line. Seems like there was always a wash to be hung out. On bright sunny days, you'd see clothes on lines throughout the neighborhood blowing in the wind. Sheets and towels dried fluffy and soft and smelled as sweet as spring flowers. Solar dryer, no electricity needed. We seldom left home except for church and school. We went to town only to purchase shoes, stockings, and under-things. Mama made all our clothes, dresses, suits, and coats, and hats. She thought the sun would harm us so she made bonnets to match our dresses. In winter, she made tams to match our coats that she made from men's overcoats, often those discarded by the neighbors. Because the wool was scratchy, she lined our coats with silk or rayon. She never purchased a sewing pattern, she created her own. First, she made a free-hand drawing on butcher paper, cut out her pattern, and placed it on the fabric. She made expert and stylish clothes for my siblings and me.

Mama did beautiful hand work, too, knitting, crocheting, and tatting, an old technique for making lace out of loops and knots. Like her mother, Mama made exquisite quilts. Before they could buy piece goods at the store, women saved leftover scraps from clothing they made for their families. One of my Grandmother's quilts was made from worn-out shirts. All that was useable were the shirttails. She'd cut the pieces into diamond shapes. She called it the Shirt-Tail Quilt. Mama's quilts were created from bits of cloth from our dresses, blouses, skirts, and nightgowns. Trying to fall asleep at night with one of her quilts over me, I looked for something she had made for me - with her love. Today, quilts are praised as works of art, both the old and the new, each as beautiful as the other.

    Family activities often centered at church. People would come for quilting bees, family games like putting together huge jigsaw puzzles, and bake sales. I remember going house-to-house selling peanut rolls for twenty-five cents a dozen, made by the ladies of the church. Ice cream suppers were held on the boulevard across the street from the church. The ladies made beautiful cakes and homemade ice cream the old fashioned way. Men folk placed ice and salt around the ice cream container and cranked the handle until the ice cream was thick. These were happy times on our boulevard - where we sat cool and shady under 100 year-old oak trees. In the fall, we gathered hickory and pecan nuts, went to sorghum mills and barn raisings in some of the old communities. Church was often the place for family Homecomings in the summertime. Box suppers were a big thing to me. The women prepared delicious food and wrapped their boxes in pretty paper and ribbons. For the auction, all the ladies would get behind a curtain and put out one foot, hoping your loving husband would recognize your shoe and choose you. Daddy never could pick out Mama's shoe. After we got home, he'd complain about the lady he had picked and her awful food. I knew Mama's shoe, why didn't he know? I guessed that children remember more about their Mama than their Dad.

    You never heard of anyone taking a vacation. People worked all the time - afraid of losing their jobs. Jobs were scarce, money was too, during the Depression years. Men had to leave their homes and families and go from town to town looking for work. Someone came to our back door just about every week. Mama would give them a hot meal and prepare a bag lunch to take on their journey to the next town. If it had turned cold and snowing, she gave them a warm shirt or coat from Dad or the boys. Many men left their homes while the weather was still warm and had no winter clothes. Mama prayed with them, asking God the Father to watch over them and help them find work. I often wondered about the men who came to our back door for food and water. Did some become lawyers, doctors, singers, poets, or writers? Each one was special in some way, just out of work looking for jobs to support their families back home. Even school children lost money in the 1929 crash - like me. At school, we were taught the values of saving money. Teachers collected our bank deposit once a week and recorded the amount in our savings book. Mine was five cents. Saving that nickel was a big sacrifice for me. I loved chocolate, but I wouldn't buy any because I wanted to have some money of my own. I don't remember my total savings, but when the banks closed, all you got was your last deposit - you know what I got. For a while, there was no money. The government issued a paper certificate, called Script. People got paid with Script and it was used for everything they purchased. Stamps were placed on the back according to what you bought. When the Script had three stamps on the back, it was turned back to whatever government agency was in charge of handling the Script.

    Mama was always willing to help others. She endured many hardships and hard times in her birth family as well as her own. As I look back, I don't see how she accomplished so much. In 1946, she was recognized for her good works and named Mother of the Year in our town. She remained a beautiful lady all her life. Her teachings are still dear to me. A time to keep:

> To everything there is a season,
> A time for every purpose under the sun.
> A time to be born and a time to die;
> A time to plant and a time to pluck up that which is planted;
> A time to kill and a time to heal...

A time to weep and a time to laugh;
A time to mourn and a time to dance...
A time to embrace and a time to refrain from embracing;
A time to lose and a time to seek;
A time to rend and a time to sew;
A time to keep silent and a time to speak;
A time to love and a time to hate;
A time for war and a time for peace.
Ecclesiastes 3:1-8

    I lived between two special families. Gertrude and Walter Reams lived on one side. They had no children, but like Mr. and Mrs. Red, they loved all the neighborhood children. Mrs. Gertrude had a beautiful garden in her back yard. I loved being with her and helped keep her garden. I pulled weeds. She had brick walkways - most everyone did - that I kept picked clean of grass and weeds. Mr. Reams worked for a wholesale drug company. He never owned a car; he walked to and from work and home for lunch each day. Thin as a rail from all that walking. One day he bought a bicycle...

    Elizabeth and Charlie Duvall lived on the other side. They had a married daughter and grandson. Their son-in-law was a colonel in the Army. Mr. Charlie had a big red barn behind their home. Along with a couple of employees, he made hand-rolled cigars. Later, he closed the cigar "factory" and purchased a grocery store on the south side of town. When his daughter and family came to visit, she would take us to Mr. Charlie's grocery. He always gave us a big sugar cookie. What a treat! Mrs. Elizabeth mostly kept house. When she wasn't busy, I would go over and visit. Duvall's had a large screened-in back porch with a ceiling fan and a swing. We'd swing and she'd tell me about places she had visited. Good place to be on a hot summer day.

I loved all my neighbors except one, Mr. Willow. He had a wife - no children. They lived in a pretty brick house with a large front porch, two rocking chairs and a swing. I never saw his wife outside the house or in the yard. When I was passing by she might come to the door to tell Mr. Willow that his meal was ready. Mr. Webb's grocery on the corner delivered their groceries. When Mrs. Willow got sick, neighbors offered help. He would only say, "We are sufficient unto ourselves." During the great flood of 1937, my Dad asked if he could take them to the edge of town so they could get help. The floodwaters had reached their front door. After Dad helped them into his boat, he said, "Not so sufficient now, are you?" No reply from Mr. Willow. We all need help sometime in our life, even if we don't want it.

Several years after his wife died, he got sick and could not care for himself. He asked Mr. Webb, who delivered his groceries, if he and his wife would move into his home and take care of him. The Webbs lived in a rented house just a few doors down from Mr. Willow. The Webbs agreed. Shortly after they moved in, Mr. Willow deeded his property to them upon his death.

Mr. Webb was a kind and gentle man. Everyone loved him. He worked in his brother's grocery store for many years. He delivered groceries to customers and neighbors who lived within two blocks of the store. They didn't have a delivery truck. He carried heavy loads in a large metal container. After the store closed, both brothers retired and Mrs. Webb retired from J. C. Penny Company.

We had two grocery stores just two blocks apart. Webb's and "the other one." Mr. Webb was kind to everyone; he'd even let you charge groceries by the week or month. Sometimes, Mama needed to buy meats from the other one. She called his hand many times because he put his thumb on the scales, as he weighed her item. She'd say, "I'm not buying your thumb today." The grocer wouldn't say a word; he'd just remove his thumb. When, I went to the grocery to pick up small items for Mama such as bread, crackers, sugar, and flour, I'd carry the purchases carefully trying not to wrinkle the paper bag because the grocer would buy them back if they were in good condition. That meant candy for my sister Ruth and me.

Mama and Dad raised flowers and vegetables in the back yard. Sometimes we went to the Market House to buy other fresh items. Farming then and now is heart- and back-breaking work. Farms that have been in families for generations are sold every year due to bad weather and foreclosures. After we left the farm in 1924, Daddy went to work for Sam Foreman. He owned the Ford Motor Company then located on Jefferson Street in Paducah, Kentucky. Dad had a mechanical mind and skills to match. In those days, people ordered Ford cars directly from Detroit. The cars arrived by rail and unassembled. It was Dad's job to put them together part-by-part at the railroad station. Then, Dad drove the new car to the Ford garage where it was readied for the owner. He worked at Ford for several years, after that he opened his own automobile repair shop and hired two men as helpers. But, when Ford built the V-8 engines, he closed his shop. His tools didn't fit the new engine and he refused to adjust to a different mechanism. Unfortunately, when he closed-out his business, he burned all the accounts receivable. He thought his customers should have paid when the work was finished or immediately after. Not good thinking, but that was the way he explained it.

Aunt Louise owned about five acres on the north side of town. She let Dad use it to plant vegetables for our family. We sold what we didn't need and it gave us some income. We even had a strawberry patch that I loved. Aunt Louise's family came from Germany and settled in this part of McCracken County. On the old charter maps, this area was called Germantown. A brother of Aunt Louise had beautiful peach and apple orchards and grew the best white corn down by the river. He let us pick what we wanted and Mama made the most delicious cream style corn from his bounty. It was really good boiled, too.

The benefits of lots of fresh foods means you have to preserve all that you can't immediately eat. Mama canned most fruits and vegetables and dried fruits on racks. She covered the drying racks with cheesecloth to keep the bugs off. Ripe fruits had to be brought inside before sundown - the night dew would ruin them.

Daddy made hominy and sauerkraut and tended more than a hundred beehives. We didn't have enough space at our house, so friends in the country let him keep some of his hives on their farms. Bees are busy. Bees keep you busy. When the super is filled, you need to put on another one. When there was a dry season and clover was not plentiful, you had to feed the bees sugar water from a container at the opening of their hive. Daddy sold honey by the frame, cut into squares, or strained and put into Mason Jars. When Mama called us in for supper, I knew how delicious the hot biscuits would be with our honey.

Mama loved flowers. Mama and Dad grew the most beautiful roses, white, crimson red, yellow, pink, and talisman. The yellow and talisman were my favorites - still are today. Mama's Dahlia's were as large as dinner plates. She raised gladiolus, hydrangea, both, pink and blue. She lined the fencerow in our backyard with sweet peas, larkspur, and snapdragons. I remember the beauty I saw when Mama's flowers bloomed. Her flowers supplied our church from spring through fall. A local florist came to Mama to purchase long-stemmed roses when he ran out of supply. So beautiful were her roses that professional growers relied on her.

You hear so much now about organic foods and green-wise technologies. I am reminded of the non-chemical produce we grew and purchased from other farmers. When you entered the market place or the neighborhood grocery, you could smell the distinctive aroma of each fruit and vegetable. When picked and purchased the same day, the taste was delicious, unlike what we purchase today that travels refrigerated over great distances - already picked green - and stored in warehouses. When today, does an apple really smell like an apple, or a peach, a peach ... tomato, or onion the same? Some say, it's only my nostalgia - that I just imagine food was tastier back then. I say, if you have not experienced non-chemically treated, vine-ripened, fresh-from-the- garden, fruits and vegetables, you may not know the difference. If we had enough produce, Mama canned all of them the same day, if not, certainly the next. Sometimes, we'd have three or four bushels to clean, hull, and peel. Ready to can, we put them in sterilized jars and then processed in a hot water bath. When we heard the "ping" we knew the jars were sealed. When they cooled, we placed them in a cool dry place in our cellar. Sadly, today the canned goods we buy have so many chemicals from liquid smoke to MSG. For many, this is a serious health hazard. Headaches and stomach upsets due to additives and preservatives make people sick - especially those in my family. Now days, you must pay more for "organic" produce - the way we farmed long ago. We did not spray harmful chemicals to deter bugs; we picked them off the plants one at a time. When Mama canned fresh foods, she used only sugar, salt, spices, vinegar, alum and sometimes grape leaves in pickles to keep the jars' content clear. We canned, dried or preserved fruits and vegetables and smoked or canned meats. Food was never wasted or discarded.

    On the Truck Farm - as we called our enterprise - Daddy planted many different kinds of vegetables. He tended a grape arbor and a big crop of Kentucky Wonder Green Beans. After canning what we'd need for the winter, Daddy packed the rest in hampers with lids and sold them to wholesalers at the freight house near the railroad station. As a small child, I remember wondering how far our green beans would travel before they reached someone's dinner table. Mama canned some of every thing Dad grew on that spot of land. Our patch was small compared to the big farms. To my delight, we shipped only a few crates of strawberries. In summer, when I was out of school, Daddy and I would leave the house around 6:00 am come back home for lunch and return to the fields until sundown. I loved watching the vegetables grow. It was hard work, but I knew I was helping my family. When the vegetables reached their bounty, I'd stay home and wash Mason Jars, zinc lids, and rubber sealing rings in hot soapy water so Mama could sterilize them for canning. Mr. Del Monte and other canneries could not compare to my Mama's products. She made gallons of delicious tomato and grape juice. Yum... nothing like a big glass of Mama's grape juice for lunch.

In the early summer, it was time for blackberry picking. Mama packed a lunch for us and away we'd go. Berries were plentiful along the roadside - so were the chiggers. You took an oilcloth with you and rubbed it on the chigger bites. If I saw a snake - I'd jump back into Daddy's truck. In other times, we'd pick all kinds of wild greens, such as, dandelion, dock, poke, Lamb's Quarters, and Crow's Foot, so called by the Cherokee because of its shape. Known to others, it was called Indian Mustard. My Cherokee ancestors passed down their knowledge of how to safely prepare wild greens. Some were poisonous and had to be picked before they bloomed. Even then, they had to be carefully prepared. Poke's roots and berries are poisonous, but if you pick them before they bloomed, cut the green tops off, par boil, drain, and rinse several times, they were safe to cook. Also, poke greens taste good in a pot of greens. Add smoked ham or bacon to the pot for lots of flavor. If you make Pot Likker Dodgers and a cornmeal dumpling, put them on top of the greens, the flavor is even better. (Pot Likker Dodgers and all recipes are located in the recipe section of this book.)

In the fall, we gathered hickory nuts, black walnuts and pecans. Mama made cakes and pies better than anyone. Two of my favorites were hickory nut pie and cake. In those days, hickory trees were plentiful in the south. Sadly, hickory trees are scarce today. So many have been cut down for firewood and Bar-B-Q pits.

MY MOTHER

My mother was the oldest of ten children. Her mother had two sets of twins. One set died after only four days. She lost the other to illness and accident. Bessie died of influenza when she was sixteen years old. Her brother, Jessie died on Christmas Day when he was only nine. He was playing on a huge pile of logs and as he neared the bottom, the logs began to roll. One crushed him. Despite his injuries, he ran to the porch and fell dead at Grandpa's feet. Mama loved Jessie so much... For many years, Christmas was a sad time for her. She was close to all her brothers and sisters.

As the oldest, she practically raised the others even as she worked in the fields. The small children went with her each day. She placed the little ones in a washtub with a quilt inside for their comfort and set them under a shade tree. Mama took a basket lunch and often made hoecakes for them. To make hoecakes, she'd make a small fire and clean the dirt from the hoe. With cornmeal and water, she made each cake, placed it on the blade of the hoe, and held it over the fire. If you make the cake thick enough, it won't slide off into the fire. After the little ones ate and fell asleep, Mama would return to the field with the hoe to weed and pick cotton. It was hard, backbreaking work. Plants grow low to the ground in tight rows and it takes small, deft hands to take out the cotton from the boll. Thorns surrounding the cotton cut into fingertips causing them to bleed and dew poison setting in. Infestations of boll weevils brought more woes.

Even as a young girl, with grown-up responsibilities, Mama cared about her grooming and appearance. She made a powder puff with moleskin. She sewed a silk cover lining on the inside and stuffed it with cotton. She caught the mole herself, cleaned and dried it! She made a toothbrush from a little stick from a sweet gum tree. She chewed the end until it was soft and used baking soda as a cleaner.

I remember the pie safe and biscuit jar in my Grandma's kitchen. She always had a cake or pie in the safe for her family and for company that might drop by. Her huge fireplace fascinated me. Guess you could say it was a combination slow cooker, Dutch oven, fryer, and bake oven. Black iron pots in different sizes hung on rods on the sides of the fireplace. She could move the pots directly over the fire or away to cook slowly or just to keep the food warm. A spider skillet could be placed on the floor of the fireplace; baked potatoes cooked in the ashes. Biscuits were cooked in a large cast iron pot with a lid and set into hot ashes. She added ashes on top or hot coals as needed and the biscuits turned out browned on top and bottom. My, her food was good!

There were all kinds of trees at Grandma and Grandpa's farm. I loved the sassafras. It's a small tree with oval leaves shaped like mittens. The smallest saplings make the best tea. First, you clean the roots and scrape off the bark. Cut into small pieces and place in the slow oven to dry out. Bring two quarts of water to boil, add a cup of roots and boil two or three minutes. Let it steep for ten minutes. Sweeten each cup with sugar or honey. Some folks say if you drink sassafras tea everyday it will help you lose weight.

Grandma and Mama knew a lot about wild plants and herbs. Their knowledge was passed down from my Great-Grandmother who was Cherokee Indian. Grandma had many wise sayings: *If the hog is killed at the wrong time, the bacon will curl. Plants that produce above ground should be planted when the moon was bright. Root vegetables should be planted when the moon was dark.* I can't remember any more, but she had many adages about life in her time. She often quoted Ecclesiastes, "to every season..." and checked the Almanac before planting. If the plants had bugs, I learned to pick them off and put in a can as I went down the rows. I continued that practice in my own gardens rather than use pesticides.

Grandma made Yellow-Jacket Soup. Yes, that's soup made from those pesky insects. The recipe came down through her Cherokee heritage. Another such recipe, she called Leather Britches. In summer, she picked and strung green beans and hung them in the smokehouse to dry. When she cooked them in the winter, they tasted like fresh green beans. (Both these recipes are found later in this book.) Grandma made jelly out of black-eyed pea hulls. She boiled, strained, measured, and put in sugar. The result looked like apple jelly. She kept a spice chest under lock and key. Spices were expensive and hard to come by. Grandma used stone crocks for canning. She had sizes from pints to gallons and used red wax to seal the lids. We used five-gallon crocks for making sauerkraut and pickles. When they were ready, Mama put them in sterilized Mason Jars with zinc lids and sealed with rubber rings.

Cousin John killed hogs in cold weather. He would always bring us a five-gallon can of lard rendered from the butchered hogs. Lard was white and pure and made the best biscuits and piecrusts. We had a root cellar for storing our canned goods to keep the jars from freezing. There were many ways to prepare food for the winter months. Fresh apples and turnips were placed in the ground with a mound of dirt and covered with straw. This way, vegetables and fruits could be banked until you needed them, cold and crisp and very tasty.

BUMBLEBEE COTTON

Grandpa and his brother had a falling out and had not been in contact for years. During the Civil War (1861-1865), Grandpa fought for the South and his brother fought for the North. Kentucky was a border state and had sympathies for both sides - or as some say, they were for whoever was winning. The sad truth is that many sons, fathers, and brothers fought against each other and families were torn apart. So, when his brother came around, I guess they patched things up. Brother had a big idea. He told Grandpa about his successful cotton farm in

Tennessee and said Grandpa should sell his farm, move down, and take up cotton growing. Grandma didn't think it was a good idea, but they packed up and moved in a covered wagon from Lola, Kentucky to Ramer, Tennessee. It must have been a long weary trip. The family dog must not have liked Tennessee because a day or so after they arrived, he couldn't be found. Several months passed and a letter came from neighbors back home in Kentucky saying that Blue, their birddog, had come back to their home place.

Grandpa tried to make a go of it, but after a few years he was through. He said, the cotton his brother bragged about "was nothing but bumblebee cotton." That means the plants were frail and grew only six to eight inches high probably due to sand-ridge soil. After all the children married and left home, Grandma and Grandpa packed up the wagon and moved back to Kentucky. Eventually, they returned to their Tennessee farm to raise livestock and corn, no cotton. Grandma tended a vegetable garden behind the house. This was about the time Mama and Daddy lost our farm. We visited them three or four times in Dad's touring car, a Ford sedan. It had two seats and canvas flaps on the sides. You had to tie them down if the weather was bad. I wish I had Mama's lap blanket, it was dark maroon and so heavy I couldn't lift it. In cold weather, she'd heat bricks and put them on the floor; we'd get in and she'd place the blanket over us. We stayed warm as toast.

After Grandpa died, Grandma came to live with us. I thought she'd stay forever; I was heart-broken when she left after only a year. She was tall and willowy. Never cut her hair. It was so long when she sat in a chair, it touched the floor. I watched her brush and brush and put it into a figure eight on the back of her head. Her complexion was dark and her eyes so brown they looked black. She was beautiful. She wore floor-length dresses with long sleeves. In cold months, she wore a pretty shawl. Her shoes were black with a strap across her foot with very little heel.

Long ago, Grandma and Mama had worn shoes with no right or left to make them last longer.

Grandma was still with us during the Ohio River Great Flood of 1937. There were many floods, but none like the Great Flood, January 1937. It surpassed all floods during the previous 175 years with damage from Pittsburgh to Cairo, Illinois. We knew winter weather up north had been severe. As the heavy accumulation of ice and snow thawed, our rivers began to rise. At the foot of our main street, the Ohio and Tennessee rivers came together and just around the bend joined the mighty Mississippi. We didn't have a floodwall at that time and no amount of sand bags could hold back the rapidly rising waters. Daddy went down to the lumber company and purchased wood and supplies to build John Boats, a flat bottom rowboat. He knew we would need a boat to get out if the water reached our house. He also made boats for our neighbors. Living on a high ridge, we could hang on longer that most communities. First, the floodwaters inundated downtown and the south side of town. These areas were not only closer to the rivers, but the land was flat. It was not long before water rushed our front door. I watched the Coast Guard come by with grab hooks to locate cars. There were only two or three cars per block. We had an Oldsmobile with a soft top. Although the floodwater ruined the car, I hated to see them punch holes in the top. Finally, we had to leave our home, Mama, Grandma, two sisters, my little nephew who was just getting over diphtheria, and me.

Daddy took us to his brother's place at the edge of town. I never wanted to say he was my uncle because he was so mean to my Dad. His wife, Aunt Louis was a saint, as I mentioned before, it was Aunt Louise who let us use her land to raise vegetables. Her husband was the Devil himself. He was always angry, cursing, and in a rage most of the time. We stayed with Uncle Devil for about a week, while Daddy would come and go to bring us food. He stayed with a neighbor who had a two-story house. Several men stayed in our neighborhood to prevent looters. It was very cold that January and the only heat they had was dry wood and coal that had been stored on the upstairs porch. The only safe way to drink water was to put in a few drops of iodine.

We couldn't take much more of this ugly old man. Daddy moved us to a little village called Water Valley down the road in the next county where we stayed in a schoolhouse. The Red Cross furnished cots, blankets, and food. Mama took a few linens - we couldn't carry much in the boat. Mama went to a hardware store and purchased a rope. She threaded the rope through the hem of the sheets and hung them to make a private place for us to dress and sleep. The Red Cross did the cooking. A nurse and doctor were on-duty during the day; the doctor went home at night. One night after supper, about everybody got sick with diarrhea, except my little nephew and Grandma. It turned out that the cook had put Super Suds (laundry soap) instead of salt in the cabbage. He said he thought it was salt. Hearing all the commotion, the nurse screamed, "Go to bed!" Well, people couldn't stay in bed and she didn't bother to find out the problem. She turned out the lights and we had to feel our way in the dark. Many people fell and got hurt. Next day, the doctor was mad at her for her cruel treatment of us. Mama later found out why the cook couldn't tell the difference between soap and salt: he was a drunk. Needless to say, he was told to leave.

In a few days, we had to move again. The school superintendent decided to re-open the schools because he thought the students had been out of school too long. From the schoolhouse, we went to a Tomato Canning Factory in another little town, Mayfield, Kentucky. Mama hung up the sheets again for our privacy. Women with children and a few Dads were placed on the second floor. We didn't have to see what was going on downstairs. Years later I learned that the first floor was for people of very low character. Police came every night to stop fights and cart the villains off to jail. The building had only two-shower stalls - and guess where they were? Mama had a large pail so we carried water to our little corner on the second floor to bathe. The Red Cross officer in charge stopped us and said, "You are not supposed to do this!"

Since he was from our town, Mama knew him. She confronted him about the goings on downstairs and about him courting the ladies-of-the-evening. From then on, someone carried water upstairs for our baths. Mr. Red Cross Officer was in charge of the cook who wouldn't let us have fresh fruit between meals that was sent there for all of us by the Red Cross. After another talk between Mama and the Officer, we had plenty of everything. He didn't want his secret courting revealed! After a week of so in the cannery, we went back home.

What a mess. The house and yard were a total wreck. There were eight inches of river mud on the floors. Daddy had already spread lime in the house and yard after he got the mud out to help kill the strains of bacteria and germs. So much cleaning - seemed like it would never end. Clean, clean, and clean some more. We lost our car, all our rugs, and some furniture. The Red Cross would replace flood-damaged furniture, but Daddy refused to accept what he thought was charity. Lots of people did accept the Red Cross offer and received all new furniture - even if they had only little more than beds, table and chairs, and a stove before the flood. Dad would only accept free food; he had no choice. We needed it. The grocery stores opened their doors and let people take what they needed. Us kids had to go to school all summer and even on Saturdays to make up the days and weeks we lost because of the flood. For us, it was good to be home in a clean place, take a real bath, and enjoy Mama's cooking. Only she could make our home shine again. Even though it has been many years ago, I know how flood victims feel. You leave your home, belongings, and treasures not knowing if you will ever see them again. God was good to us and my little nephew got well. I loved him dearly. I thought of him as my little brother, playmate, and friend.

Many tales have been told about people's lives during the Great Flood. One story stands clear in my mind. There was a lady who gave birth to a daughter just before she was rescued from the floodwaters consuming her home. Her baby was wrapped in several blankets. In helping mother and child into the rescue boat, the baby was dropped into the cold water. Miraculously, the baby floated. She was in the water only a few seconds before being rescued. The mother named her Wadda Flood Denna. Her story made headlines after the floodwaters subsided and the local newspaper was back in operation.

GROWING UP

George Scott said, "If you're not from Kentucky, you're just hangin' over the edge." Native sons and daughters take pride in Kentucky's wild game, hickory-smoked ham, bacon, and Bar-B-Q, tobacco, sorghum, corn, bourbon, and the Kentucky Derby. The Derby race is always held the first Saturday in May. In my day, men wore straw hats and snappy shoes with spats. It didn't matter what the weather was that day. Cold and rainy or hot and sunny, it was a day for parties, Mint Juleps, and river boat rides on the Belle of Louisville or Delta Queen. There were plenty of beaten biscuits, country-smoked ham, Bar-B-Q, and large kettles of Burgoo, a stew made with about fifteen pounds of short beef ribs, six or eight large hens, maybe a squirrel or two, and at least eighty pounds of root vegetables per kettle. The pot cooks all day. Burgoo was made at other times during the year for church groups and political rallies.

Daddy smoked hams, bacon, and sausage. Mama made muslin sacks on her Singer Sewing Machine. For the sausage, she packed two pounds into bags ready to be smoked. She seasoned it just right. When ready, it was oh so good! Some men folk thought Daddy's home brew was good, too. The most famous beverage in Kentucky is corn whiskey. Made in families for generations from plenteous crops of corn, sweet water, and land rich with limestone. Making home brew was considered respectful if you stayed within the law. Mama didn't approve of Daddy's enterprise.

Mama made lye soap for washing clothes, sheets, and towels. After hanging out for an hour or so, they were white as snow and smelled like sunshine on your bed. One day in 1932 or 1933, Mama hung out the wash as usual. As she went in and out of the house to hang the laundry on the clothesline, she noticed the wet clothes and linens dripped with streaks of mud. There was no rain or rain clouds. She could not imagine what caused the mud and the dark clouds that blocked the noonday sun. A day or so later, the local newspaper reported that the huge cloud blocking the sun was from a dust storm in Oklahoma. Soon after another dust storm blew in from Kansas. It was called Black Sunday Blizzard. Dust darkened the skies and fell on towns and cities east as far as New York City. Families in the dust bowl - as we later knew it - were left with nothing, their farms destroyed, people and livestock died. No water, no food, no livelihood. Many destitute families headed for California only to die on the way or arrive with dreams of a better life shattered.

Mama cooked on a wood stove until 1948. On Sunday, before we went to church, she'd cook a big dinner and leave it in the warming oven over the stove. We came home to fried chicken with milk gravy, hot biscuits or buttermilk cornbread, creamed potatoes, green beans, and wilted lettuce in summer. In winter, she would add a vegetable she had canned in the summer or fall. For dessert, she made banana pudding or chocolate cake. We loved them all as they changed from time to time. Everything we ate was made from scratch. There were always plenty of jams, jellies, apple butter, pickles, relish, and all kinds of canned fruits and vegetables. Mama worked hard from daylight until dark. Summers were hot. Canning on a wood stove made the kitchen extremely hot. Mama's kitchen was a place of comfort. At suppertime, you could smell what she was cooking, long before you opened the front door. In early morning, we'd wake-up to the aroma of hickory-smoked, country ham and biscuits.

Ice and milk deliveries were made to each home by horse-drawn wagons. A card place in the window showed the amount of ice you needed. Colors on the cards were green, red, white, and black, representing the blocks of ice at 25, 50, 75, or 100 pounds. Us children enjoyed meeting our friendly iceman. He's chip off a piece of ice for each one of us. We'd jump up and down; it was so cold to hold it in your hand. Our milk was left at the front door. In winter when it was cold and freezing, the cream on top would push off the cardboard cap. Dairies used glass bottles in those days. Milk was pasteurized, but not homogenized. It was after World War II that milk was stored in cardboard cartons.

Doctors made house calls back then. When I was four-years-old, I had diphtheria. Young as I was, I remember being so sick. Dr. Goodloe came and treated me with an anti-toxin serum. It was weeks before I could go out to play. He would never take any money for his calls. He loved Mama's cooking - " she's the best cook in town." He ate lunch with us most everyday. Daddy kept his car in good working condition in payment for his services.

Mama could do anything. She had a keen mind, strength of purpose, and concern for the wellbeing of her family and neighbors. Our lives were made better by her remarkable skills, imagination, and dedication. One of her children, my sister Ruth, older than me by two years contracted infantile paralysis, polio, soon after she was born. Mama said she was so tiny, she could hold her in the palm of her hand. Ruth's left hand, arm, and leg were most affected and she couldn't walk. About the time she was five-years-old, Mama took her to the Cripple Children's Clinic in Louisville, Kentucky where doctors fitted her with leg braces. After many months, she began to take a few steps. We were so proud of her. In time she was able and ready to go to school with me. Ruth wasn't shy like me. She was then –and all her life - spunky. If she didn't agree with you, an argument broke out. At recess, I'd take a chair from the classroom to the playground and find a safe spot for her - in the shade if it was hot weather. I would swing and jump rope all the time keeping an eye on her. Some of the children at recess were cruel to her because of her handicap.

They would turn her out of her chair - knowing she couldn't get up - or they would hit her. No matter if the kids were bigger than me, they had a fight on their hands. I protected Ruth all her life...

Mama and other mothers came to our school to cook lunch. They took turns and no pay. After Mama finished her work at home, she walked to school rain or shine, cold or snowing. She was always there to do her part. I was happy to see her there in the kitchen, serving her good cooking to all the kids – and me. As a young child, I didn't realize how much time and effort it took her so we could have tasty, healthy, hot meals at school. For some children, it was their only good meal.

I loved Christmas. Mama made it special by her cooking and baking. She made jam cakes with caramel icing, fresh coconut cakes, fruit pies, and divinity candy with black walnuts. She baked turkey with her special dressing and all the trimmings. If Dad had been hunting, we had wild duck or geese. (Mama saved the down for pillows and feather beds.) Daddy hunted quail too. As long as I can remember, we had fried quail, milk gravy and buttermilk biscuits on Christmas morning. Added to that were honey, sorghum molasses, and homemade jellies with sweet butter. Delicious!

Another treat was our Christmas oranges. Mama would roll them to soften the juice. Then, she would cut a hole in the top for us to place a peppermint stick. We used it like a straw to get out the sweet orange juice.

Dad, Mama, Ruth, and I would pile in our truck - Dad named it "Blue Haven." She had a rumble seat and so much fun to ride in. Later, he took out the rumble seat and made it his service truck. For our Christmas tree, he drove the "Blue Haven" to a friend or relative's farm, chopped down a cedar and brought it home. It made the house smell like Christmas. To this day, fresh cedar reminds me of Christmas. Dad made the tree stand out of lumber scraps and secured the tree in it. On Christmas Eve, we decorated our tree. Some families used candles, but we didn't for fear of fire. We used whatever we had to make the tree beautiful. We'd string popcorn and cranberries, make ornaments, hang streams of paper icicles, and place a white sheet around the bottom. My older sister would send Ruth and me a telegram from Santa Claus telling us he was in the sleigh and on his way from the North Pole to see us. She was thoughtful of others, especially family. As a teen-ager, she operated the elevator at the Taylor Office Building at 4th Street and Broadway. With her first pay check, she bought Mama a dress, I think it was her first dress from a department store.

Department stores gave customers high-quality service. The counters throughout the stores were beautiful. Merchandise was attractively displayed in cases made of wood with glass tops and fronts. The sales ladies wore white gloves when they waited on you. Lingerie and stockings were kept in boxes with tissue paper and you asked to see your size and color. I remember the creaky wood floors and big ceiling fans at our department stores and drug stores. We had family-owned grocery stores and drug stores in our neighborhood. If you needed dry-cleaning or laundry service, it was picked-up and delivered to your door. Mr. Robinson owned the icehouse and made daily deliveries in his horse-drawn wagon. It seems everybody knew everybody in our town. Daddy went hunting with Mr. Robinson for deer and bear. In front of his ice-house, Mr. Robinson put a small bear in a cage. One time it grabbed a small child. The child wasn't hurt, just scared. Some said he was teasing the bear. Anyway, the city officials asked him to get rid of the bear.

Dad had lots of men friends. Fishing the rivers and creeks was always good and the woods and bottomland were full of wild game, turkey, hog, squirrel, rabbit, coon, quail, duck, and geese. Often, Dad hunted with a little old farmer named Mr. Moses who lived in two-room house with Rudy, his dog. They went everywhere together. Mr. Moses never married. He lived to be over 100-years-old. As long as he was able to keep up his farm, he raised vegetables and sold them from his stall at the Market House.

Not far from Mr. Robinson's Ice House, the Market House was a trade center for surrounding farms. Farmers brought in their fruits, vegetables, and flowers for sale according to the season. I could smell the wonderful fragrances of the flowers a block away - or so I thought. Farmers backed their wagons up to the stall they had rented for the year. Each uncovered their produce, set up the scales, and got ready for business. Market opened at 6:00 am and by 11:00 am everybody was sold out. I went with Daddy to Market and other stores nearby. Michael's Hardware store was one of my favorite places. Mr. Michael had everything under the sun. I remember he had a repair-kit for Mama's aluminum pots. We couldn't afford to replace them with new ones so we went to Michael's and the repair kit worked fine. Pot would never leak again.

When I walked to town with Mama, we passed a Milliner's Shop, owned by two French ladies. In front of their house, they had a large, wooden display case built on legs with glass on three sides and a mirror in the back of it. We stopped to admire their lovely hand-made hats. They made hats for gentlemen and ladies. I wondered how they came all the way from France to our community.

MY TOWN

In the 1930's and 1940's, McCracken County was the strawberry capital of the world. Our strawberries were the sweetest. After all the strawberries were picked and shipped away, our town had a celebration street dance. At the end of the season, a Strawberry Queen was selected. The queen and her royal court were featured in a grand parade. If the farmers couldn't get enough employees during berry picking season, kids could be excused from school to help. Young girls used their berry-picking money to get their hair curled. They earned twenty-five cents a handy (six boxes). Along with other girls, I decided to get a "Strawberry Perm" so called because the beauticians gave more perms during this season. I got one - and only one for a lifetime. The perm apparatus looked like something I imagined out of Frankenstein's story. Picture this, a floor-lamp like pole attached to a large hood - connected to several dangling electric cords with metal clips at the end - attached to metal hair rollers placed in my hair by the beautician. I think she thought the perm had set when she smelled burning hair, "she's fried." "Afro" is the only way I can describe my hair-do; although this was not a hairstyle we knew back then. Before the perm, I had long beautiful black hair. To my horror it had to be cut short so there wasn't so much to break off. I thought my hair would never grow out. Mama soothed me by saying it won't be long before it is all grown back. Daddy made me some big hair curlers from an empty Calumet baking powder can. He cut into strips with his ten snips and I covered the strips with a soft cloth and rolled my hair around it. I didn't want my scalp to be damaged like my hair. Mama knew I wanted curly hair like her, my two sisters, and one of my brothers. She probably knew the perm wasn't a good idea. Sometimes, mothers let their children find out such things on their own. As my hair grew out, I had soft curls.

    The last strawberry festival took place in 1941. We had little news of Hitler's rampage across Europe until Japan bombed the Navy Base at Pearl Harbor. We learned that shipyards were being built around our coastlines and ammunition depots were under construction in several states. America was at war with Japan and Germany. Restrictions were placed on what you could buy and how much. We were issued Ration Books for everything from shoes to sugar. Manufacturing went into high gear for the war effort. People said even Lucky Strike cigarettes went to war - the color on the package was changed from green to red - because the color green was needed for the war. Families experienced even greater sacrifices when news of loved ones wounded, missing, or killed in action reached them. So many of my classmates left and didn't return. One of the saddest tragedies to hit our town was when an Army troop train carrying boys we knew crashed and caused many casualties. On the same day, another train headed in the opposite direction carrying Navy recruits. It arrived safely at its destination, carrying my young husband.

With so many young men away, there were not enough workers for the big farms. Wives and mothers, children and old folks planted small vegetable gardens on rooftops and yards they could tend themselves. Called them, Victory Gardens in honor of their soldiers, sailors, and pilots in harm's way.

After the war, there were many changes in my world. Young people would never again pick the strawberry farms. Some thought it would be fun to pick berries, but soon learned it was back breaking work that farmers and their own children pickers long endured. Without a willing and cheap labor force, U-Pick signs began to appear at all the large farms. Even the telegraph man on his bicycle was seen no longer. When he came down our street, I knew he had news of a wedding, birth, death, or someone on their way to visit. When our streetcars were replaced by city buses I took my little nephew on the first bus ride - several times - from the north to the south side of town. On the first day, the round trip was free. After that, the fare was a nickel.

Every town has its stranger-than-fiction stories, including mine. I was about seven or eight-years-old when one of our banks was robbed. The police shot and killed one of the gangsters. I don't know why, but after he was embalmed, they put him in a pine box and displayed him on the courthouse lawn! It seemed like the whole town turned out to see - my Daddy took me too. No one ever claimed the body, so he was buried in a pauper's grave in one of our cemeteries. Several years later by the time I was a teenager, a new funeral home was built. Several of my girl friends and I went to the "open house" event - I guess that's what you'd call it. The Director showed us around and there in one of the rooms was a plaster-of-Paris cast: "This is the gangster killed during a bank robbery."

People knew that John Dillinger had a hideout in southern Illinois about sixty-miles from our town. Was this robber with Dillinger's gang?

Another strange-but-true-story is about Charles "Speedy" Atkins. In May 1928, poor Speedy went fishing and fell into the Ohio River and drowned. His body was turned over to Hamock's Funeral Home for a pauper's burial, but Mr. Hamock decided to try out a new super preservative instead. The process turned Speedy's body into a mummified-wooden-state. It preserved his facial features and turned his dark skin a reddish color. Mr. Hamock didn't bury him, but put him on display at the funeral home where Speedy remained until he washed away during the 1937 flood. Later, he was returned to the funeral home as a "flood victim." After Mr. Hamock died in 1949, his wife took "custody" of Speedy and eventually had him buried in Maplelawn Cemetery, in 1994, sixty-six years after he died. Speedy's story has been told on the Discovery Channel and recorded in Ripley's Believe It or Not. Speedy even traveled to Burbank, California and appeared with Mrs. Hamock on the Johnny Carson Tonight Show. Speedy made no comment...

THEN AND NOW

In 1815, Paducah was called Pekin. It was a mixed community of American Indians and white settlers. Chickasaw Chief Paduke welcomed the people who came down the Ohio and Tennessee rivers. All shared goods and services and cultures until William Clark of the Lewis and Clark expedition arrived in 1827 with a deed from the US government to take the land. Clark told the Chief and his people to leave the area. They moved south to Mississippi. When the new town was established, General Clark renamed it Paducah, in honor of the Chief. Clark invited Chief Paduke to return for the ribbon-cutting ceremony. Sadly, on his way back by boat, the Chief died of malaria.

Being a river town back in the 1800's, there were several hotels constructed of wood with porches across the front. I remember when the last one was torn down. Workers found the skeleton of a young lady inside a trunk in the attic. She had on a hoop skirt, fashionable in the 1800's. Evidence showed that she had been shot and stuffed inside the truck. Had she been one of the dance hall girls? The history of these towns along the rivers tells about life on the busy waterfronts. Boats brought in goods and supplies, gambling boats docked for business, steamboats carried passengers, and the railroad yards flourished.

During the Civil War, General Ulysses S. Grant and the Union Army took possession of the town and it remained occupied for the duration of the war. General Lloyd Tilghman, a native son of Paducah, was killed at the battle of Vicksburg, Mississippi. His death marked thirty-five years after Chief Paduke and his people arrived in Mississippi. They were among the American Indians displaced to Oklahoma on the Trail of Tears.

Winters were colder then. Even the Ohio and Tennessee rivers would freeze over. People from nearby counties drove their wagons across the thick ice for a much shorter trip to town to buy supplies. In later years, the winters were not so cold so the rivers froze only half way. Today, it is a rare occasion.

Lots of changes came about in the early 1900's, including the kitchen. New products such as Crisco replaced lard and Oleo Margarine replaced butter. I remember Oleo, as white as snow, came in a 1-pound box with a small packet of yellow coloring. When thoroughly mixed, it looked just like butter. Electric appliances, like hand-held mixers, made some cooking tasks easier. Store-bought cookies, especially my favorite to this day, Oreo cookies, became available. Piggly-Wiggly opened the first self-service grocery store in 1916. The first hamburger stand opened in Wichita, Kansas, so they say. White Castle, a fast-food franchise, began to show up in larger cities. They sold hamburgers for a nickel. Depression era foods, including macaroni and cheese and chipped beef on toast, remained popular. Roadside diners became a common sight along the highways.

We got our first radio in 1936. All of us crowded around it for news and weather and the National Barn Dance on Saturday night broadcast from Chicago, Illinois. I remember listening to Lum and Abner, Amos and Andy, The Inner Sanctum, The Lone Ranger, Our Miss Brooks, and many more.

I was in Virginia recently. We visited Mount Vernon, George Washington's home and George Mason's home, Gunstan Hall. Seeing and reading about these historic sites caused me to realize that this way of life ended with my generation. For two hundred and fifty years, people had farmed, preserved, and prepared food in much the same ways: smoking meats, drying apples, peaches, and pumpkin, storing apples and turnips in the ground, canning in stone crocks - like my mother and grandmother. George Mason's family had mattresses filled with straw – like the straw mattresses we had with feather beds of goose and duck down on top. I am grateful we survived hard times. It is truly God's amazing grace that we came through all kinds of hardships. It was because of my mother that our lives turned out well - with smiles of happier times to come. She was a special lady and her heart was full of love for us.

My oldest brother, Robert built a racecar - he would never let me ride in. He became an automobile mechanic and later Service Manager at the Paducah Ford Motor Company until it closed. He married an angel, Thelma whom I loved dearly. My oldest sister, Mabel worked at the Taylor Building. She married Ed, a young engineer who came from the Peabody Hotel in Memphis, Tennessee to the Irvin Cobb Hotel in Paducah. They had a son. As a boy, my brother Paul delivered newspapers and worked for the Gilbert Bennett Drug Company with stores at Fourth, Fifth, and Sixth Streets at Broadway. Paul later worked for Kentucky Utilities. He drove a bus all over town with a large supply of table and floor lamps and sold more lamps than any other salesman. He married Polly and had two sons. They moved to California where Paul continued successfully in sales. My brother, Charles was a talented athlete in high school. He went on to work for Coy "Shortie" Stacy in the restaurant business. Charles married Helen and had two sons and a daughter. My sister Ruth, just two years older than me, had polio and was never able to work or marry. As for me, I married the love of my life, Dan, and I had a daughter and a son. We were together for over sixty-six years until he passed away.

Now, I live a long way from Kentucky. I think about my home at different seasons of the year, especially the fall. I miss the changes of the leaves after a cold front passed through - the bright orange, yellows, and reds were particularly stunning. I always loved the maple, hickory, and sweet gum trees and the smell of burning leaves. We didn't know then that the burning might be harmful to the atmosphere. There were late fruits and vegetables ready for canning. The scent of fresh dill still reminds me of Mama preparing pickles. I loved the magnificent sight of geese and ducks returning to our cornfields and lakes on their way down from Canada. When they took flight - as if some commander gave the order - the sky darkened and the sounds of hundreds of beating wings and honking water birds filled the air.

Sometimes it saddens me to think of the days I loved and enjoyed as a young girl that are no more. What I miss most today is my Mama and the friendly, caring neighborhoods that were a big part of my life for a very long time. I will always remember the joys of my childhood and I will treasure these sweet memories as I continue my journey.

Keep them all. Life is precious.

LaVerne M. Littleton

I REMEMBER...
COOKING SECRETS

Here are some rarely known tips passed down from my Grandmother Peak, Mama, Bessie, and many other great cooks who have shared their secrets with me.

To help prevent cake layers from sticking to pans, place the pans on a wet towel as soon as they come out of the oven.

To keep buttered cake pans from sticking, substitute powered sugar for flour when preparing the pans.

To keep chocolate cakes brown on the outside, grease pans and dust with cocoa instead of flour.

For creamier and smoother fudge, add one-teaspoon cornstarch to each cup of sugar used in making fudge.

Cooking eggs in boiling water will produce less leathery eggs. To cook hard-boiled eggs, bring to a boil, cover and remove from heat. Let eggs sit for 15 minutes.

If you have leftover grits, press into a tall glass. Store in refrigerator overnight. For breakfast the next day, slide the grits from the glass and cut into 1/2-inch round slices. Fry in bacon grease. Serve with bacon and eggs.

Freeze flour before making piecrust. This keeps it very cold when mixing. Use ice water to make the dough and handle it as little as possible.

Use cream cheese instead of shortening for a key lime piecrust. It will be less flaky and add flavor to the pie.

To keep meringue from weeping and shrinking, add a teaspoon or tablespoon of unflavored gelatin to meringue mixture.

Rinse a pan in cold water before scalding milk to prevent sticking.

For party sandwiches, freeze bread before cutting into fancy shapes. Spread with filling while bread is stiff.

When preparing party sandwiches for freezing, spread first with butter (never salad dressing) then spread with filling. No more soggy bread.

Add a pinch of baking powder to powdered sugar icings. Icing will not get hard or crack and will stay moist.

To open a coconut more easily, place in a warm oven.

For a different dessert, caramelize sweetened condensed milk: boil a can - unopened - of sweetened condensed milk in water enough to cover for 3 hours. Store in refrigerator and do not open until ready to use. Serve over pound cake or ice cream.

Whip egg whites with a little sugar before folding into cake batter.

For skimming excess fat from soup or gravy, wrap several ice cubes in a piece of cheesecloth and skim along the surface. The fat will congeal and cling to the cloth.

You can keep a roast or poultry from sticking to the bottom of your cooking pan by using celery stalks to form a rack in the pan. Celery will add moisture and flavor.

Melt chocolate quickly by wrapping in aluminum foil and placing in a small pan over low heat.

Put sugar cubes in a cheese container to keep cheese free of mold.

Add 1-cup cooked rice to meat loaf. It will be moist, slice firmly, and taste new.

Use crushed potato chips instead of breadcrumbs when you make a meat loaf.

Raisins will be more evenly distributed if heated in oven before being added to cake batter.

A few tablespoons of instant mashed potatoes will thicken stews.

When cutting up dried fruit, such as raisins, dates, or apricots, oil the knife or scissors.

You can make 1-ounce unsweetened chocolate by combining 3-tablespoons of cocoa with 1-tablespoon melted butter.

I REMEMBER...
MAMA'S HEALING REMEDIES AND TREATMENTS FOR SICKNESS

Vinegar has been used to fight against infections for centuries. Over 3000 years ago, the Egyptians used date palm vinegar as a healing property. Hippocrates, the father of medicine, prescribed vinegar for curing persistent coughs. During the American Civil War, vinegar was used as a disinfectant on soldiers' wounds.

...eated a sprained ankle with vinegar. She cut a brown paper bag ...... strips and dipped them in moderately hot water and vinegar. She added just a bit of cayenne pepper to the mixture before she wrapped the ankle with the strips.

For nausea, Mama dipped a cloth in warm vinegar and placed it on the sick one's stomach. She kept replacing the warmed vinegar cloth until the patient felt better.

Arthritis was treated with a combination of 1-teaspoon vinegar and 1-teaspoon honey added to a glass of warm water. Take 2-times a day. Taken 3-times a day before meals helped get rid of fat and serves to suppress appetite.

The Greeks and Romans used a similar mixture for dietary and medicinal purposes. *Posca was a drink popular in ancient Rome and Greece, made by mixing sour wine or vinegar with water and *flavouring herbs. It originated in Greece as a medicinal mixture but became an everyday drink for the Roman army and the lower classes from around the 2nd century BC, continuing to be used throughout Roman history and into the Byzantine period. It was made by reusing wine spoiled by faulty storage and had important dietary advantages. As well as being a source of liquid, it provided calories and was an antiscorbutic, helping to prevent scurvy by providing vitamin C. Its acidity killed harmful bacteria and the flavouring helped to overcome the bad taste of local water supplies.*" [1]

*And honey, according to other sources

Showalter, Dennis E. *Soldiers' Lives Through History*, pp. 36-37. Greenwood Publishing Group, 2007. ISBN 0313333483

For a sore throat, Mama gave us vinegar with salt in a glass of hot water - as hot as we could tolerate - to gargle as needed.

Mama set a large pan with vinegar and warm water under the bed of the patient. This helped kill the germs in the sick room.

Mama used Vick's Ointment for dry skin, especially for the feet. She combined Vick's Ointment with Mentholatum rubbed on the chest and throat. Then she covered the areas with a hot flannel cloth, replacing as the cloth cooled. This relieved a sore throat, cough, and bronchitis.

I REMEMBER WHEN...

People were thrifty and repaired rather than throw away the way we do today. In my early-married years, I repaired my husband's jackets, turned his shirts, and mended his socks.

We made old shirts look like new. When the collars and cuffs wore out, we turned them over and made new buttonholes and changed the buttons to the opposite side of the shirt.

We patched socks and had our shoes repaired. The tops were made of good leather so we only needed new soles and heels to get more wear out of them.

Mama repaired our bed sheets. When the middle was thin and worn, she would tear the sheet apart and sew the outside edges together. Then she hemmed the worn part on each side to keep it from raveling. Even aristocrats in the estates of Europe and Great Britain had their employees mend sheets by this method.

I REMEMBER FIRSTS...

Kool-Aid was first sold in 1927, by mail order.

Sliced bread was first sold in our town in 1928.

Bird's-Eye frozen foods arrived in 1930. In the same year, Teflon by Dupont, the electric mixer, and the pressure cooker were new.

Bisquick was introduced in 1931.

In 1934, Nabisco introduced Ritz Crackers, named for the luxury hotel.

Food service on passenger airplanes began on American Airlines' DC-3's.

Garbage disposal was invented in 1943.

Tupperware was introduced in 1946.

In 1947, Aluminum Foil became available and the first boxed cake mixes were sold in supermarkets.

The Kitchen Aid dishwasher was introduced in 1949.

FAMILY RECIPES FROM KENTUCKY IN THE 1800'S

BEVERAGES

Lynn's Moonshine Eggnog

This is a pre-Civil War recipe from Kentucky passed down to my Dad. There's an old saying about testing moonshine to see if it's fit to drink. Pour some 'shine on a concrete sidewalk and light it with a match. If you get a blue flame, it's good to drink. If you get a yellow flame, don't!

5-dozen eggs, separated
5-pounds sugar
6-quarts milk
4-quarts Whisky or Moonshine
Ginger, ground
Nutmeg, ground

Beat egg yolks until light and fluffy. Gradually add sugar. Mix well after each addition. Add milk, then whisky. Beat egg whites until stiff, but not dry. Place egg whites on top of eggnog. Sprinkle with ginger and nutmeg to taste.

Mint Julep

Reverend Andrew Reed, an English traveler, wrote that he first encountered the Mint Julep at a tavern in Kentucky in 1834. He found its popularity already overwhelming and its mystique full-blown. Bourbon is Kentucky's oldest industry thus earning the state its reputation as the Bourbon Capital of the World. President John Tyler often served Mint Juleps to Heads of State on leisure afternoons at his Virginia Plantation.

2 ½-ounces Woodford Reserve Kentucky Bourbon
2-teaspoons spring water
1-teaspoon powdered sugar
Shaved ice
Fresh mint

Muddle 4 sprigs of mint with a wooden pestle. In a frosted pewter tankard, combine Woodford Reserve Kentucky Bourbon, spring water, powdered sugar, and mint. Fill with shaved ice and gently stir. Top with mint leaves. Sip...slowly, through a short straw.

Legend has it that a farmer in Kentucky always stored his whiskey in white oak barrels in his barn. One day lightning struck and set the barn afire. His whisky barrels stored below were charred. Not willing to discard his prime brew, he later discovered that the charring improved the flavor of his whiskey. This event took place in Bourbon County. That's how Bourbon whiskey got its name and distinctive flavor.

Sassafras Tea

3-Sassafras sticks about 4 inches long
3-cups water
Sugar
Cream

Place sassafras sticks in pot with 3-cups water. Bring to boil Simmer for one hour. Add sugar and cream to taste.

SOUPS

Yellow-Jacket Soup
A long-forgotten Cherokee Nation recipe...

Gather Yellow-Jacket combs (nests). Carefully pick out all grubs, keeping them intact. Put the grubs in the oven on a pan to let them brown. After browning, add them to water, a little grease and salt.

VEGETABLES

A big pot of spring greens - wild lettuce, dandelion greens, violet leaves, mustard greens, poke, and turnip greens - was most welcomed served with Pot Likker Dodgers.

Pot Likker Dodgers

2-tablespoons minced green onions, chopped with a small amount of tops

1 & ½-cups cornmeal, un-sifted

1-egg

½-teaspoon salt

¼-teaspoon pepper

Stir in enough boiling Pot Likker from greens to cornmeal, green onions, salt and pepper to make stiff dough. When slightly cooled, thoroughly mix in 1-egg. Take this by spoonfuls and shape into small patties about ½-inch thick. Lay gently on top of simmering greens. Cover and cook about 10 to 14-minutes or until done.

Kraut
A Pre-Civil War recipe.

Peel off outer layers of cabbage. Wash and cut out core. Shred cabbage with kraut cutter. Layer cabbage salting each layer. Fill to the top of a stone crock. Put on lid and weigh down with a rock or brick. Leave about 12-days. During this time, skim off scum every other day. Pack into sterilized quart jars with a teaspoon salt. Process in a canner by the hot water method.

Hominy

My Dad made hominy in an old ash hopper used by his father.

Hickory wood ashes
Hot water
Shelled corn
Salt

First, make the lye out of ashes from hickory wood. Next, put ashes in the hopper and pour hot water over ashes. The lye drips out through a hole in the bottom of the hopper. Boil shelled corn in the lye. Cook until skins and eyes come off. Wash several times to make sure all the lye washed away. Cook several hours in fresh water until tender and doubled in size. Can in jars quart-size. Put 1-teaspoon salt in each jar. Use the hot water method to seal jars.

Clabbered Cheese

My Grandmother and Mama made this cheese.
It was good for bouts of colitis and diarrhea.

Clabbered (sour) milk
Cheesecloth bag

Made from sour milk, clabbered cheese was first heated near the fireplace to separate the curd from the whey. Then, it was poured into a cheesecloth bag and hung over a pan to drip. This was called smearcase or cottage cheese.

Corncob Jelly
A recipe from my Grandmother Peak.

12 to 13 large red corncobs
Heavy white cloth for straining
Water
3-cups sugar
Pectin

Place corncobs in a pan and add enough water to cover. Boil 30-minutes. Take off stove and strain in a heavy cloth. You need 3-cups of cob juice. If needed, add more water to make this amount. Add 3-cups sugar and bring to full boil for 2 to 3-minutes. Add a package of pectin. Cook as directed on the box or until it reaches the jelly stage. Pour in sterilized jars. Tastes like apple jelly. Red cobs give it the color.

Black-Eyed Peas Jelly
Similar to the Corncob Jelly recipe.

Fresh-shelled black-eyed peas
Water
Sugar
Pectin

Take the husks from fresh-shelled black-eyed peas. Boil and strain. Add sugar and pectin. It comes out almost clear. Looks like and tastes like apple jelly.

Leather Britches
This is my Grandmother's recipe for preserving green beans.

Fresh green beans
Large needle
Strong white thread
Water
Ham hock or smoked bacon

Cut off ends of green beans. With a large needle and strong white thread, run the string close to the middle of the beans. Allow some space between each one. Grandmother kept them in the smokehouse until dried and ready to cook. Beans will change color and shrivel some while drying. Cover with water and soak over night - like any other dried beans. Drain and add fresh water and a ham hock or smoked bacon. Cook until tender for about 20 to 30-minutes. Taste like fresh green beans.

DESSERTS

Election Cake

President Abraham Lincoln's wife, Mary Todd had this cake prepared in celebration of his re-election and the end of the War.

1-cup sugar

2 ¾-cups sifted flour

½-teaspoon salt

¼-teaspoon mace

1-teaspoon cinnamon

1-egg

1-teaspoon lemon rind, grated

2-teaspoons lemon juice

1-cup currants, soaked in whiskey overnight (or 8 hours)

1-tablespoon sugar

¾-cup scalded milk

1-package yeast

¼-cup warm water

1-cup flour

½-cup butter

Scald milk, add 1-tablespoon, sugar. Dissolve yeast in warm water. Add to milk. Add un-sifted flour and beat until well blended. Let rise in warm place until it doubles in size. Cream butter and sugar until light. Drain currants from whiskey. Place sifted flour, salt, mace, and cinnamon in sifter. Add egg to creamed mixture and beat until light. Stir in lemon juice and rind. Add yeast mixture and beat thoroughly. Add currants. Sift in flour. Add whiskey. Beat well. Place in prepared pan. Cover. Set aside in warm place. Let rise until it doubles in size. This will be slow – up to 6 hours!

Bake at 350-degrees for 45-minutes. Cool. Turn out on cake rack.

Prepare Orange Glaze:

Combine 1-cup confectioners sugar, sifted with ½-cup orange juice. Brush cake with orange glaze.

Brandied Peaches

In late summer, pick the best ripe peaches. Peel and put in a large size Mason jar. Place a layer of peaches, a layer of sugar and continue to fill the jar. Not too full so to put the lid on tight. Dig a deep hole in the ground below the freeze line and bury the jar with straw around it. When winter comes, dig it up and enjoy the peaches with a sip of the peach brandy.

BREAKFAST

Praline French-Toast Casserole
By permission from Paula Deen, Simon & Schuster.

Generously butter 13-x 9 x 2-inch casserole dish.

8-eggs, slightly beaten
1 & ½-cups half & half cream
⅓-cup maple syrup
⅓-cup light brown sugar, packed
10 to 12-slices challah or soft bread

Mix eggs, half & half, maple syrup, and sugar in a large bowl. Place bread slices in the prepared casserole dish and cover with the egg mixture. Cover with plastic wrap and place in the refrigerator overnight. Next day, preheat oven at 350-degrees. Remove casserole from refrigerator.

Prepare topping:

½-cup butter (1 stick)
½-cup light brown sugar, packed
⅔-cup maple sugar
2-cups chopped pecans

Melt butter in a saucepan. Add sugar and maple syrup. Cook 1 to 2- minutes. Stir in pecans. Pour the mixture over the bread and bake 45 to 55- minutes. Allow dish to set for 10-minutes before serving.

Breakfast Rolls

Preheat oven at 325-degrees.

Prepared greased 13 x 9 x 2-inch baking dish.

2, 1-pound loaves frozen bread dough, thawed
1-cup brown sugar, firmly packed
1, 5 & ½- ounce package regular vanilla pudding
½-cup melted butter

¼-cup half & half
½-cup pecans, chopped and divided
½-cup raisins, divided

   Cut 1-loaf of dough in small pieces. Place in the greased baking dish. Combine brown sugar, pudding mix, butter, and half & half. Mix well. Drizzle half the brown sugar mixture over bread dough pieces. Sprinkle ¼-cup nuts and ½-cup raisins. Cut second loaf into small pieces. Place over first layer. Drizzle remaining brown sugar mixture over dough pieces. Sprinkle with remaining nuts and raisins. Cover and refrigerate overnight. Bake at 325- degrees for 50 to 60-minutes.

Sausage Balls
Preheat oven at 400-degrees.
Set out cookie sheet, do not grease.

2-cups Bisquick
2-cups shredded cheddar cheese
1-pound bulk sausage
1-cup apple, peeled and grated

   Mix all ingredients. Roll into small balls. Place on cookie sheet. Bake at 400-degrees for about 15-minutes. Drain on paper towel. Makes about 50.

Fluffy Baked Omelet
Preheat oven at 350-degrees.
Set out 9-inch skillet.

6-eggs, separated
1-tablespoon flour
1-tablespoon cornstarch
1-cup milk
2-tablespoons butter
½-teaspoon salt
Black pepper

Beat egg yolks. Add flour, cornstarch, salt and pepper. Beat until smooth. Gradually add milk, beating constantly. Beat egg whites until stiff but not dry. Fold into egg mixture. Melt butter in a heavy 9-inch skillet. Pour in egg mixture. Bake at 350-degrees for 20-minutes. Fold onto hot platter. Serve immediately. Serves 6.

Date and Orange Muffins
Preheat oven at 400-degrees.
Prepare buttered muffin tins.

1-whole orange
½-cup orange juice
½-cup dates, pitted, chopped
1-egg
½-cup butter or margarine
1 & ½-cups flour
1-teaspoons baking soda
1-teaspoons baking powder
¾-cup sugar
1-scant teaspoon salt

Cut orange into pieces. Remove seeds and drop pieces into blender. Blend until rind is finely ground. Add juice, dates, egg, and butter and give another whirl in the blender. Sift dry ingredients into bowl. Pour orange mixture over dry ingredients and stir lightly. Drop by spoonful into 18- buttered muffin tins. Bake at 400-degrees for 15-minutes.

Coffee Cake
Preheat oven at 300-degrees.
Prepare a greased 11 x 7 x 1 & ½-inch baking pan.

½-cup butter or margarine
1-cup sugar

2-eggs, well beaten
2-cups cake flour
2-teaspoons baking powder
½-teaspoon salt
½-cup milk
1-teaspoon vanilla
¼-cup melted butter or margarine
1-cup brown sugar, firmly packed
1-teaspoon ground cinnamon
1-cup chopped pecans

     Cream ½-cup butter and 1-cup sugar until fluffy. Add eggs. Mix well. Combine flour, baking powder and salt. Sift and set aside. Combine milk and vanilla and add alternately with flour mixture to creamed butter and sugar mixture. Mix in electric mixture set on low speed. Pour into greased baking pan. Spread melted butter evenly over batter. Combine brown sugar and cinnamon and sprinkle over batter. Top with pecans. Bake at 300-degrees for 40 to 45-minutes. Cool in pan 10-minutes before serving. Yield: 12 servings.

Christmas Coffee Cake Ring
Preheat oven at 350-degrees.
Set out Bundt pan.

1-package frozen dinner rolls
1 & ½-sticks margarine
½-cup brown sugar
1-jar each of red and green cherries
1-package pecan halves
1-cup sugar
1-teaspoon cinnamon

     Melt ½-stick margarine with ½-cup brown sugar in bottom of Bundt pan. Arrange nuts and cherries. Melt 1-stick margarine in small frying pan. Mix 1-cup sugar and 1-teaspoon cinnamon. Roll each dinner roll in margarine, then sugar, then cinnamon mixtures. Sprinkle nuts and cherries as you build the rolls. They will rise to the top of the pan. Cover and leave in refrigerator over night. When removed from the refrigerator, let rise in a warm place. Bake at 350-degrees for 30-minutes. Let coffee cake set 15-minutes before turning out on a large platter.

French Breakfast Puffs

Preheat oven at 350-degrees.
Grease 28-small muffin tins or 10-regular sized.

⅓-cup soft margarine or butter
½-cup granulated sugar
1-egg
1 & ½-cups sifted flour
½-teaspoon salt
¼-teaspoon nutmeg
1 & ½-teaspoons baking powder
½-cup milk
6-tablespoons melted margarine
½-cup sugar
1-teaspoon cinnamon

Mix margarine or butter, sugar, and egg. Sift together flour, baking powder, salt, and nutmeg. Stir in alternately with milk. Fill small, greased muffin tins ⅔-full. Bake 14 to 16-minutes at 350-degrees. Melt 6-tablespoons butter. Mix ½-cup sugar with 1-teaspoon cinnamon. Remove from oven and immediately roll in butter mixture, then sugar mixture.

If you use 10-regular size muffin tins, bake at 350-degrees for 20 to 25-minutes.

Cheese and Raisin Bread

Preheat oven at 350-degrees.
Prepare large greased cookie sheet.

½-cup sugar

½-teaspoon salt

2-packages active dry yeast

3 & ½-cups all purpose flour

6-tablespoons butter or margarine

⅔-cup water

1-egg

1-egg white

    In a bowl, combine sugar, salt, yeast, and 1-cup flour. In a saucepan, heat butter and water until very warm (120 to 130-degrees). With electric mixer at low speed, beat liquid into dry ingredients. Beat mixture 2-minutes at medium speed. Stir in 1 & ¼-cups flour. On a flowered surface, knead dough about 8-minutes. Add about ½-cup flour while kneading. Shape dough into a ball. Place in a greased bowl. Turn the ball over to grease the top. Cover. Let rise about 1-hour in a warm place (80 to 85-degrees) until doubled.

Prepare cheese and raisin filling:

1, 8-ounce container creamed cottage cheese

1, 8-ounce package softened cream cheese

½-cup confectioners sugar

1- teaspoon grated lemon peel

1 egg yolk

½-cup raisins

    In a bowl, press cottage cheese through a fine sieve. With electric mixer at low speed, beat cottage cheese with creamed cheese and confectioners sugar, grated lemon peel, and egg yolk, until smooth. Stir in ½-cup raisins. Refrigerate filling.

Combine dough and filling:

Punch down dough, turn onto floured surface and cover. Let rest 15-minutes. With rolling pin, roll dough into 15 x 12-inch rectangle. Spread filling into 4-inch strips lengthwise down the dough's center. Cut dough on both sides of filling strips - crosswise - into 1-inch strips. Place strips at an angle across the filling by alternating each side in a braided pattern. Place braid on greased cookie sheet. Cover. Let rise until doubled. Beat egg white and brush over braid. Bake at 350-degrees for 20-minutes or until brown. Cool 15-minutes before serving.

Strawberry Jam & Cheese Loaf

Preheat oven at 350-degrees.
Prepare lightly greased baking sheet.

1-package dry yeast
½-cup warm water (105 to 115-degrees)
2 & ½-cups Biscuit Mix
1-tablespoon sugar
1-egg, beaten
1, 8-ounce package cream cheese
⅓-cup sugar
1-tablespoon lemon juice
¼-cup strawberry preserves

Dissolve yeast in warm water. Let it stand 5-minutes. Add Biscuit Mix, sugar, and egg. Stir well. Turn out dough onto a flowered surface and knead until smooth and elastic. Place dough into a well-greased bowl. Turn over to grease top. Cover and refrigerate 8-hours. Punch down dough and turn out onto a lightly greased baking sheet. Roll into a 14 x 16-inch rectangle.

Combine cream cheese, ⅓-cup sugar, and lemon juice. With electric mixer set at medium speed, beat until smooth. Spread mixture 2-inches wide - lengthwise - down center of dough. Make 3-inch cuts into dough at 1-inch intervals on long sides. Fold and overlap strips - diagonally - over filling in a braided fashion. Cover and let rise in a warm place (85-degrees) free of drafts. Let stand 45-minutes or until double in bulk. Bake at 350-degrees for 20-minutes. Remove from oven and spoon preserves down the center. Return to oven and bake an additional 5-minutes. Remove from oven and let stand 10-minutes before serving. Yield: one 14-inch loaf.

Dutch Baby Pancakes
From my niece, Connie Martin.
Preheat oven at 425-degrees.
Set out iron skillet or 2 to 3-quart size pan.

¼-cup butter
¾-cup milk
¾-cup flour
½-teaspoon salt
1-tablespoon sugar
½-teaspoon vanilla extract
3-eggs

    Melt butter in skillet or pan at 425-degrees. Mix eggs, milk, flour, salt, vanilla, and sugar in a blender set at high speed for 2 to 3-minutes. Pour batter into pan. Bake 20-minutes. The middle makes a perfect crater for a filling.

Prepare filling:
2-cups sliced strawberries with sugar, or
4-6 fresh peaches with brown sugar and a few drops of almond flavoring
4-tablespoons butter
¼-cup honey
Dash of cinnamon or nutmeg

In a heavy skillet, melt butter and lightly sauté prepared fruit. As it softens, drizzle honey, brown sugar or white sugar over the fruit. Add a dash of cinnamon or nutmeg. Cook fruit until just heated and tender, but not mushy. When pancake is done, spoon hot fruit in center. Sprinkle with sifted powdered sugar.

Banana Treats

2-bananas
Flour
1-egg
1-2 tablespoons milk
Japanese Panko breadcrumbs
¼-cup sifted powdered sugar
¼-teaspoon cinnamon
Hot oil

Cut bananas, diagonally. Beat 1-egg with milk. Dip banana slices in flour, egg mixture, and breadcrumbs and fry in hot oil. Mix sifted powdered sugar with cinnamon. Sprinkle over bananas while hot.

Huevos Rancheros

6-eggs
6-canned tortillas
1 & ½-cups chopped onion
1-garlic clove, minced
½-cup bacon fat
4-tomatoes, peeled and chopped
¾-cup finely chopped hot peppers
½-teaspoon salt

Sauté onion and garlic in ¼-cup bacon fat for 5-minutes. Add tomatoes, hot peppers, and salt. Cover pan and simmer 10-minutes. Remove cover and simmer 10-minutes. Meanwhile, sauté tortillas in remaining ¼-cup bacon fat for 30-seconds on each side. Remove and keep hot. Fry eggs in remaining fat in skillet. Put 1-egg on each tortilla and spoon sauce over it.

Danette's Curried Fruit
Preheat oven at 350-degrees.
Set out 1 & ½-quart casserole dish.

1-large can peaches, drained
1-large can pears, drained
1-large jar cherries, drained
1-large can diced or chunk pineapple, drained
⅔-cup sliced apples (pie-type)
4-tablespoons curry powder
¾-cup light brown sugar
⅔-stick butter

Place drained fruit in a 1 & ½-quart casserole dish. Combine curry powder with light brown sugar and butter. Melt over low heat and spoon over fruit. Bake covered 1-hour at 350-degrees. Refrigerate. Before serving, reheat for 20-minutes at 350-degrees.

SOUPS & APPETIZERS

Cream of Navy Bean Soup

2-cups Navy Beans
5-cups beef broth (5-cubes plus 5-cups hot water)
2-cups onion, chopped
3-tablespoons butter or margarine
3-tablespoons flour
2-cups milk
1-cup cream
½-teaspoon seasoned salt
¼-teaspoon black pepper
½-teaspoon paprika

Wash beans and soak over-night in water to cover. Drain beans and put into a large, heavy saucepan. Add broth and onion to saucepan, stirring well. Cover and simmer for about an hour until beans are soft and mushy. Force bean mixture through a sieve or food mill and set aside. Heat butter in large saucepan. Stir in flour and cook until mixture bubbles and browns lightly. Remove from heat and add milk gradually while stirring constantly. Return to heat and continue to stir. Bring to rapid boil and cook for 1 to 2-minutes longer. Stir in bean puree, cream, seasoned salt, pepper, and paprika. Heat thoroughly, stirring constantly. Garnish with minced parsley. Serve with cornbread.

Beef Stew

1-pound boneless round steak
¼-cup all purpose flour
¼-teaspoon pepper
¾-cup chopped onion
3-cups water
½-cup carrot, finely chopped

¼-cup celery, finely chopped
2-tablespoons minced parsley
½ teaspoon salt
⅛-teaspoon dried whole thyme
2-cups potatoes, cubed
1-cup sliced carrots
1-cup onion chopped
1-cup frozen green peas, thawed

  Trim fat from meat and cut into 1-inch cubes. Combine flour and pepper. Dredge meat in flour, reserving the excess. Cook meat, onion, and reserved flour mixture in oil in a Dutch oven over low heat until meat is lightly browned. Add water and the next 5 ingredients. Cover and reduce heat. Simmer 1 & ½-hours. Stir in potato, carrot, onion and cover. Simmer for 20-minutes. Add peas. Cook an additional 10-minutes. Yield: 6-servings at 1 & ½-cups each.

Cream of Leek Soup

4-cups sliced leeks, all of white part and some of green tops
4-cups diced baking potato
5-cups water
1 & ½-teaspoons salt
⅔-cup, or more, of sour cream

  Bring leeks and potatoes to a boil. Add salt and lower heat. Simmer for 20 to 30-minutes. Purée only ⅔ of soup. Whisk in sour cream and simmer just a moment.

Lamb Stew

2-pounds lamb stew meat, cut into 2-inch pieces
2 & ½-teaspoons salt
¼-teaspoon black pepper
¼-teaspoon sweet basil

¼-teaspoon marjoram

1-small bay leaf

1-teaspoon grated lemon peel

3-tablespoons lemon juice

2-tablespoons brown sugar

4 & ½-cups potatoes, diced

2-cups carrots, sliced 1-inch thick

2-large onions, sliced

3- stalks celery, cut into 1-inch slices

1, 10-ounce package frozen green peas

     Combine lamb with salt, pepper, basil, marjoram, bay leaf, lemon peel, and lemon juice in a large pot. Add water to cover. Place over medium heat and bring to a boil Cover and reduce heat. Simmer 4 to 5-minutes or until lamb is almost tender. Remove excess fat from surface. Stir in brown sugar, potatoes, carrots, onions, and celery into mixture in pot. Cover and bring to a boil. Cook over low heat for 35 to 45-minutes or until vegetables are tender. Add frozen peas 15-minutes before cooking is complete.

APPETIZERS

Shrimp Dip

2-tablespoons boiled shrimp, chopped
½-cup celery, chopped
½-cup onion, chopped
1-cup mayonnaise
1 & ½-tablespoons lemon juice
16-ounces cream style cottage cheese
Salt to taste

    Mix all ingredients, except cottage cheese, until well mixed. Next, add cottage cheese and stir. Refrigerate over night. Serve with Wheat Thin crackers, fresh raw vegetables, or use as a sandwich spread.

Beer Cheese

1-pound cheddar cheese
2-cloves garlic, finely minced
¼-teaspoon cayenne pepper
¼-teaspoon Tabasco Sauce
1-can stale beer set out several hours

    Let cheese stand at room temperature. Mix ingredients well. Add stale beer. Consistency should easily spread on crackers. Keep covered and store in refrigerator.

Spinach Dip

1-package frozen spinach, uncooked
¼-cup parsley, chopped
½-cup onion, chopped
1-teaspoon salt
½-teaspoon pepper
2-cups mayonnaise
Tabasco Sauce to taste

Thaw spinach and squeeze out all liquid. Mix all ingredients in blender. Serve with fresh vegetables, carrot sticks, celery, and cauliflower.

Summertime Dip

1-cup mayonnaise
¼-cup chili sauce
½-cup ketchup
1-small onion, grated
1 & ½-teaspoon dry mustard
1-teaspoon black pepper
Paprika and Tabasco Sauce to taste

Combine all ingredients in a jar and shake until mixed well. Chill 4-hours. Serve with raw vegetables or cold boiled shrimp.

Dill Dip for Veggies

⅓-cup sour cream
⅔-cup mayonnaise
½-teaspoon Worcestershire Sauce
1-teaspoon onion, minced
1-teaspoon seasoned salt
1-teaspoon fresh dill, finely chopped
1-tablespoon fresh parsley, finely chopped

Mix all ingredients. Chill overnight. Serve with any fresh vegetables.

Chili Dip

1-can chili, without beans
1, 8-ounce package cream cheese
1, 4-ounce can chopped green chilies, drained
1, 2 & ½-ounce can sliced black olives

Combine chili and cream cheese over low heat until cheese melts, stirring occasionally. Stir in chilies and olives. Serve warm with any large chips. Makes 3-cups.

Chili Oil

¾-cup peanut oil
1-tablespoon cayenne pepper, ground

Place oil in saucepan. Stir over medium heat until hot. Remove from heat and add ground pepper. Strain oil through clean cloth, two times.

Party Mix
Preheat oven at 250-degrees.
Select large cookie sheet, 1-inch deep.

2-cups Corn Chex
2-cups Rice Chex
2-cups Wheat Chex
2-cups Cheerios
2 cups pretzel sticks
1-can mixed nuts
1-cup margarine
2-tablespoons Worcestershire Sauce
1 & ½-teaspoons Lowery's Seasoned Salt
½-teaspoon Tabasco Sauce
½-teaspoon chili powder
½-teaspoon garlic powder
½-teaspoon onion salt

Melt margarine in a skillet. Add seasonings. Mix together and pour over Chex, Cheerios, pretzels, and nuts. Place on cookie sheet and bake 1-hour at 250-degrees. Stir about every 15-minutes.

SALADS, DRESSINGS, & SAUCES

My Mama's Potato Salad
Made best from leftover mashed potatoes.

6-white potatoes
1 & ½-sweet onions, finely diced
5 - 6 hard-boiled eggs, chopped
2-tablespoons cider vinegar
Salt and pepper to taste

Mix potatoes until light and fluffy. Add the next 3-ingredients. Mix well. Save 1 hard-boiled egg slice it and add on top for decoration.

Sweet Potato Salad

3-sweet potatoes, peeled and cubed
1-medium red apple with peel, core and cut into cubes
½-cup pecans, chopped

Cook sweet potato cubes in water with ¼-teaspoon salt until tender. Do not overcook. Drain and cool. Add apples and pecans.

Mix ingredients together for
Vinaigrette Dressing:
3-tablespoons extra-virgin olive oil
3-tablespoons vegetable oil
3-tablespoons rice vinegar
½-teaspoon Dijon Mustard
½-teaspoon salt
½-teaspoon black pepper

Combine all ingredients in a jar with cover and shake well. Makes about ⅓-cup dressing. Pour over salad when ready to serve.

Potato Salad

2-pounds medium potatoes (about 6)

Cook potatoes in enough water to cover. Bring to a boil. Cover and cook 25 to 30-minutes until potatoes are tender. Drain. Cool slightly, until easy to handle. Peel and cut into bite size chunks.

Mix the following ingredients in a large bowl:

½-cup mayonnaise

½-teaspoon salt

2-teaspoons apple cider vinegar

2-teaspoons onion, minced

1-teaspoon prepared mustard

⅛-teaspoon black pepper, more if desired

¼-cup milk

1-cup celery, thinly sliced

Mix mayonnaise, salt, vinegar, onion, mustard, pepper, and milk. Stir in potatoes and celery (pimento pepper, if desired) adding milk until desired consistency. Use a rubber spatula to gently mix potatoes with dressing. Serve on lettuce leaves or cover and refrigerate for later.

Mandarin Orange Salad

6-ounce package of orange gelatin

1-cup of boiling water

1-pint orange sherbet

1-can of mandarin oranges, drained

1-cup heavy cream, whipped

Dissolve gelatin in boiling water. Fold in orange sherbet. Place in refrigerator for 1-hour. Remove and stir in mandarin oranges and heavy cream.

Strawberry Pecan Salad

1-small can crushed pineapple
1, 6-ounce package strawberry gelatin
1, 8-ounce whipped topping (Cool Whip)
1-cup pecans, chopped
1, 8-ounce carton cottage cheese, small curd

    Heat pineapple over medium heat for 5-minutes. Add gelatin. Next, add pecans, cottage cheese, and whipped topping. Chill overnight.

Congealed Cucumber Salad

1, 3-ounce package lemon gelatin
1-cup boiling water
1-tablespoon onion, finely chopped
1-teaspoon vinegar
½-pint cottage cheese, small curd
¼-cup mayonnaise
1-cup cucumber, finely chopped

    Dissolve gelatin in water, and vinegar. Let stand until syrupy. Beat cottage cheese and mayonnaise with a whisk. Add cucumber and onion. Stir. Chill until firm.

Tomato Aspic

1 & ¼-tablespoons unflavored gelatin
2-cups tomato juice
2-tablespoons lemon juice
1-teaspoon sugar
¼-teaspoon salt
1-teaspoon Worcestershire Sauce
½-stalk celery, finely chopped

    Soak gelatin in ¼-cup tomato juice. Heat remaining juice to boiling and pour over the gelatin mixture and stir until dissolved. Add lemon juice, salt, sugar, and Worcestershire. When slightly thickened, add celery, place in mold and chill.

Shelley Green Bean Salad

1-can Shelley Green Beans or regular green beans
1-can cut wax beans
1-can red beans
½-cup vinegar
⅔-cup sugar
½-cup vegetable oil
½-cup onion, chopped
½-cup red bell pepper, chopped

Drain green beans well. Rinse and drain red beans. Combine the next five ingredients and pour over beans. Toss gently. Marinate for several hours or overnight. Serve with slotted spoon. Yield: 6 to 8 servings.

Mabel's Pasta and Cheese Salad

3-cups pasta (elbow, small penne or shells)
1-cup mayonnaise
¼-cup sweet milk
1-cup sour cream
2-teaspoons French's Mustard
2-tablespoons apple vinegar
½-teaspoon salt
¾-cup celery, chopped
¼-cup red bell pepper, chopped
¼-cup sweet onion, chopped
2-cups cheddar cheese, cubed in small pieces

Cook pasta according to package directions. Cool. In a large bowl, mix cooled pasta, cheese, celery, red pepper, and onion. Next, mix mayonnaise, milk, sour cream, salt, mustard, and vinegar. Toss this over pasta and cheese mixture. Chill well before serving.

Sea Foam Salad

1, 14-ounce can pear halves
1-cup pear syrup
1, 3-ounce box lime gelatin
6-ounces cream cheese, softened
2-tablespoons milk
½-cup heavy cream, whipped

     Drain pears, reserving 1-cup of the syrup. Mash pears with fork. Heat pear syrup and pour over lime gelatin stirring 2-minutes until dissolved. Beat cream cheese with milk until smooth and blended. Gradually beat in hot gelatin. Chill until slightly thickened. Fold in pears and whipped cream. Chill in 1 & ½-quart mold until firm. Remove from mold and serve on salad greens. Serves 8.

Virginia Taylor's Cranberry Salad
1972 Christmas Bazaar
Grace Episcopal Church
Paducah, Kentucky

3-cups fresh cranberries
2-medium navel oranges
2 & ½-cups sugar
½-teaspoon salt
¼-cup lemon juice
3-envelopes unflavored gelatin
½-cup cold water
1-cup boiling water

     Grind cranberries and whole seeded oranges. Add sugar, salt, and lemon juice. Dissolve gelatin in cold water. Add boiling water to gelatin. Mix well. Add cranberries and oranges. Chill in two 8 x 8 x 2-inch pans.

Cucumber & Tomato Salad

3-medium tomatoes, sliced
2-medium cucumbers, thinly sliced, do not peel
¼-cup apple cider vinegar
¼-cup vegetable oil
3-tablespoons mayonnaise
2-tablespoons sugar
½-teaspoon salt

Combine tomatoes, cucumber slices, and onion rings in a large bowl. Set aside. Combine vinegar, vegetable oil, mayonnaise, sugar, and salt. Beat, using wire whisk, until smooth. Pour dressing over tomato mixture. Toss gently. Cover and chill at least 2-hours, stirring occasionally. Serve with slotted spoon. Yield: 6 servings.

Peach Salad

1, #2-½-size can sliced Freestone peaches
⅔-cup cottage cheese
½-cup pecans, chopped
1-cup peach syrup
1-package lemon gelatin
½-cup whipping cream

Drain peaches, reserve 1-cup peach syrup. Heat syrup and pour over gelatin. Stir until dissolved. Chill. Add cottage cheese and chopped pecans into thickened mixture. Fold in sliced peaches. Beat whipping cream until stiff. Fold into gelatin mixture. Pour into a mold that has been prepared with salad oil. Chill until firm. Garnish with mayonnaise and pecan halves. Serve on crisp greens.

Seven-Cup Salad

1, 8-ounce carton sour cream
1, 8-ounce carton cottage cheese, small curd
1, 3-ounce package orange gelatin
1-cup fruit cocktail, drained
1-cup mandarin oranges, drained
1-cup mini marshmallows
1-cup coconut, grated
1-cup pecans, chopped

Mix dry orange gelatin to sour cream and cottage cheese. Add fruit, marshmallows, coconut, and pecans.

Seven-Layer Salad

1-head lettuce, chopped
1-large bell pepper, chopped
1-cup celery, chopped
1-large purple onion, chopped
1-package frozen LeSieur English Peas, cooked until just tender
6-boiled eggs, sliced circular
2-cups mayonnaise, mixed with 2-tablespoons sugar
Parmesan cheese, shredded
Cheddar cheese, shredded
Mozzarella, shredded
Bacon bits

Layer ingredients in glass bowl, in order listed above. Seal tightly. Refrigerate several hours before serving.

German Potato Salad

3-pounds potatoes
¼-pound bacon
½-cup sugar

¼-cup flour
1-tablespoon salt
⅛-teaspoon black pepper
½-cup white vinegar
1-cup water
½-cup celery, chopped
¼-cup onion, chopped
¼-cup green peppers, chopped (optional)

      Boil potatoes until done, but firm. Cool, peel, and cube. Fry bacon until crisp and set aside. Place ¼-cup bacon fat in a skillet. Stir in sugar, flour, salt, and pepper. Add vinegar and water. Cook until thick, about 5- minutes. Add celery, onion, and peppers to cubed potatoes. Pour hot dressing over potato mixture and mix lightly. Crumble bacon on top. Serve warm.

Stuffed Mushrooms

Preheat oven at 400-degrees.
Prepare buttered baking dish.

1-pound fresh mushrooms
2-tablespoons butter
2-tablespoons vegetable oil
4-green onions, chopped finely
2-cloves garlic, crushed (optional)
3-tablespoons parsley, chopped finely
¼-teaspoon salt
¼-teaspoon pepper
2-tablespoons lemon juice
¼-cup half-and-half cream
¼-cup bread crumbs.

      Wash mushrooms under cold water. Pat them dry on paper towels. Remove stems from caps and save for later. Sauté caps in hot butter for

2-minutes on each side until lightly browned. Place caps, hollow side up, in a buttered baking dish. Add oil to skillet. Chop mushroom stems finely, combine with green onions, garlic, and parsley and season with salt and pepper. Sauté in oil and butter for 5-minutes. Add lemon juice and cream. Simmer 5-minutes more. Fill cups with this mixture and top with breadcrumbs. Bake 5-minutes at 400-degrees just before serving. Serve on buttered toast.

Sunshine Sauce

1, 10-ounce jar pineapple preserves
1, 10-ounce jar apple jelly
1, 1 & ½-tin dry mustard
1, 5-ounce jar horseradish, drained
1, 8-ounce package cream cheese
1-teaspoon cracked red pepper

Combine preserves, jelly, mustard, and horseradish. Mix thoroughly and pour over cream cheese. Keep refrigerated. Serve with crackers.

Basic French Mustard

⅓-cup English mustard, dry
¼-teaspoon salt
1-tablespoon sugar

Mix above ingredients well.
Beat 2-whole eggs. Add ⅔-cup white wine vinegar. Mix with dry ingredients. Cook over medium heat until thick. Cool.

You may wish to try one of following options to this basic recipe: 4-teaspoons honey, mashed black olives, anchovies, tarragon, or green pepper corns.

Beer Batter for Fish

Pat fish dry. Sprinkle on both sides with lemon juice. Let stand 15-minutes. Combine 1-cup flour and 1-teaspoon salt. Set aside. Combine 1-cup flour, 1-tablespoon paprika, 1-tablespoon salt, and 1, 12-ounce can of beer. Stir until well blended.

Dredge fish in flour and salt. Dip into beer batter. Fry until golden brown in ½-inch oil, heated to 370-degrees. Garnish with watercress and lemon wedges. Batter can be stored for 3 to 4-days in refrigerator until ready to use.

Thick Cream Sauce

3-tablespoons butter
¼-cup flour
1-cup hot milk or light cream
Salt and pepper to taste

Melt butter in heavy saucepan. Stir in flour and cook over low heat, stirring constantly, for about 2-minutes. Do not let flour brown. Gradually add hot milk, stirring until sauce thickens, about 3-minutes. Remove from heat. If sauce is to be held for later use, cover with wax paper to prevent skin from forming on surface. Makes 1-cup.

Medium White Sauce

2-tablespoons butter
2-tablespoons all-purpose or instant blending flour (Gold Medal)
1-cup warm milk
Salt and pepper to taste

Melt butter in heavy saucepan over low heat. Blend in flour. Cook 3 to 4-minutes, stirring constantly. Remove from heat before you add milk. As you add milk, stir constantly with a whisk. Return to low heat, stirring constantly, for about 6 to 8-minutes or until thickened. Add salt and pepper. Makes 1-cup.

Bar-B-Q Chicken
Miles Merideth's Recipe
McCracken County, Kentucky

Miles cooked chicken and ribs for political rallies, church suppers, and school picnics throughout the county.

Prepare sauce:

1-gallon apple cider vinegar
1-pound lard
1-pound butter
Small can ground black pepper
Small can cayenne pepper (mild) or red pepper (hot)
¼-cup salt

Mix ingredients above and bring to boil. Meanwhile, prepare charcoal fire until coals are red hot.

Prepare chickens:

You need small, whole chickens. Have the butcher cut each in half. Lightly salt chicken on both sides. Place chicken breast side up on the grill. When it starts to bubble, Dip in sauce and turn other side over on the grill. When chicken begins to get dry, dip in sauce and turn over again. Continue until you have turned the chicken 3 to 5-times. Dip again and place in a covered container. Set for 15-minutes or more to let the chickens steam.

Paul's Bar-B-Q Sauce

1-quart apple vinegar (5% acidity)
1-cup canned tomatoes
1 & ½-cup tomato purée
½-stick butter
½-stick margarine

1 & ½-tablespoons ground red pepper
1-tablespoon black pepper
6-tablespoons granulated sugar
1-tablespoon brown sugar
½-tablespoon paprika
3-tablespoons salt
3-cloves garlic, finely chopped
¼-cup onion, chopped

    Add 2-teaspoons flour to a little of the vinegar before combining all the ingredients. Cook on a low boil for 30-minutes. Strain mixture through a sieve so it will be smooth.

My Mama's Tomato, Cucumber, & Onion Salad

¼-cup apple cider vinegar
1-teaspoon salt
¼ to ½-teaspoon black pepper
2-tablespoons vegetable oil (Canola)

    Combine the first 4-ingredients. Mix well. Add oil and shake until well blended. In a medium bowl, layer tomatoes, cucumbers, and sliced sweet onion.

Mustard Vinaigrette

4-tablespoons Balsamic vinegar
2-teaspoons Dijon Mustard
Salt and ground pepper
¼-cup extra virgin olive oil
½-tablespoon finely minced shallots (optional)

    In a small bowl, whisk together vinegar and mustard. Add salt and pepper to taste. Gradually whisk in oil. Refrigerate. Just before serving, whisk again.

Basil Vinaigrette

1 & ⅓-cups olive oil
⅔-cup white wine vinegar
¼-cup fresh basil, finely chopped
1-teaspoon salt
½-teaspoon black pepper

    Combine all ingredients in a jar. Cover tightly and shake. Chill. Just before serving, shake well again. Toss dressing with salad greens.

Honey Orange Vinaigrette

¾-cup vegetable oil
¼-cup apple cider vinegar
2-tablespoons honey
¼-teaspoon fresh ground pepper
¼-teaspoon poppy seeds

    Combine all ingredients in a jar. Cover tightly and shake vigorously. Serve over fruit or green salad greens.

Honey Lime Dressing

1-cup oil
⅔-cup honey
⅓-cup sugar
⅓-cup lime juice
1-teaspoon grated onion
1-teaspoon paprika
½-teaspoon celery seeds
½-teaspoon salt
½-teaspoon Tabasco Sauce

    Blend ingredients for a few minutes in a blender. Serve over grapefruit or orange salad.

Sour Cream Dressing

1-cup sour cream
½-cup apple vinegar
¼-cup sugar
1-teaspoon salt
¼-teaspoon pepper

    Blend all ingredients well.

Russian Dressing

½-cup Thousand Island dressing
1-tablespoon caviar
1-teaspoon chives, chopped

    Mix all ingredients well.

Honey Dressing

⅔-cup sugar
⅓-cup honey
5-tablespoons vinegar
1-teaspoon onion juice
1-teaspoon dried mustard
1-teaspoon paprika
¼-teaspoon salt

    Mix all ingredients. Slowly add 1-cup of salad oil. Serve with fresh fruit.

Tartar Sauce

½-cup mayonnaise
½-onion, chopped and squeezed in cheesecloth until dry
1-dill pickle, chopped and squeezed out all liquid
4 to 5-capers, chopped

    Mix well. Serve chilled with fish or shrimp.

Cocktail Sauce

½-cup chili sauce
⅓-cup ketchup
½-tablespoon Worcestershire Sauce
2-tablespoons lemon juice
Horseradish and Tabasco, according to taste

   Mix all ingredients and chill.

Dill Sauce for Fish

2-tablespoons dill, chopped
1-teaspoon dill seed
2-tablespoons parsley, chopped
2-tablespoons lemon juice
1-teaspoon salt
Pepper to taste
1-teaspoon paprika
⅓-cup melted butter
1, 3-pound salmon, mackerel, or halibut

   Make dill sauce by combining dill, dill seed, parsley, lemon juice, salt and pepper with melted butter. Spread half the sauce on one side of fish. Broil on a foil-lined rack for 15-minutes. Turn fish. Spread the other side with remaining sauce and broil 15-minutes or until done. Serves 6.

Easy Hollandaise Sauce

2-egg yolks, slightly beaten
2-3-tablespoons lemon juice
1-stick cold butter (¼-pound)

   Place in a saucepan and cook over low heat, stirring constantly, until butter melts and sauce is slightly thick. Season to taste with salt. Makes 1-cup sauce.

Fruit Dressing

½-cup sugar

1-teaspoon dry mustard

1-teaspoon salt

1-cup salad oil (vegetable oil)

3-tablespoons vinegar

2-teaspoons poppy seeds

1-tablespoon lemon juice

1-teaspoon paprika

      Combine all ingredients except oil. Add oil a little at a time, mixing with a wire whisk. Yield: 1 & ½-cups.

VEGETABLES

Turnip Greens

Wash 4-pounds of turnip greens, trim, and cut into 1-inch strips. Place greens in a pot with 1-cup water and 2 to 3-cubes chicken bouillon cubes. Cook down until tender and most of the water is cooked out. Add a package of fresh spinach. Mix together well and cook about 15 to 20-minutes longer.

Okra Fritters

¼-cup cornmeal
¼-cup all purpose flour
½-cup onion, finely chopped
½-cup evaporated milk
1-large egg, lightly beaten
3-tablespoons fresh parsley, chopped
2-tablespoons Parmesan cheese, grated
½-teaspoon salt
¼-teaspoon cayenne pepper
2-cups fresh okra, sliced (frozen okra, thawed, can be used)
Vegetable oil
Extra salt

Combine first 9-ingredients, stir in okra. In Dutch oven, pour in oil 2-inches deep. Heat to 350-degrees. Drop mixture by tablespoons into oil. Cook until golden brown. Turn only once. Drain on paper towel. Sprinkle with salt. Serve immediately. Yield: 4 to 6-servings.

Cucumbers in Sour Cream

1-large cucumber, pared and thinly sliced
¾-tablespoon salt
Vinegar

½-cup dairy sour cream
1-tablespoon sugar
¼-teaspoon dried dill weed
Dash of pepper

    Arrange cucumber slices in shallow dish. Sprinkle with salt. Add vinegar to cover. Let stand at least 30-minutes. Drain. Combine sour cream, sugar, dill, and pepper. Toss with cucumber slices. Chill 1-hour. Makes 1 & ⅓-cups.

Mama's Vegetable Gumbo

2-cups fresh okra, sliced
2-large red tomatoes, peeled and chopped, about 2 cups
2-cups fresh white cream corn (cut off kernels and scrapes milk from cob)
Salt and pepper to taste
1-cayenne pepper, chopped (if you want it hotter)

    Place ingredients in Dutch oven pan with bacon drippings in the bottom. Cook over medium heat. Stir often to keep from scorching. If you need more liquid, add just a little water. Not too much it you like the gumbo thick. Cook until vegetables are tender. Taste to see if you need more salt or pepper.

Suggestions: Fresh vegetables are best, but you can use frozen okra. To cut corn kernels from cob, stand ear of corn over the middle of a Bundt pan. As you scrape, the kernels will fall into the pan.

Sweet Potato Surprise

2-cups cooked sweet potatoes
½-teaspoon salt
1-egg
8-large marshmallows
½-cup crushed cornflakes

Mash cooked potatoes. When partly cool, add beaten egg and salt. May need to add a little milk. Flour hands and form sweet potato mixture around a marshmallow to make a ball. Roll in crushed cornflakes. Heat vegetable oil hot enough to brown a bread cube in 40-seconds. Fry sweet potato balls in vegetable oil until brown. Drain on paper towel.

Bourbon Sweet Potatoes
Preheat oven at 375-degrees.
Grease a baking dish.

4 to 5-medium sweet potatoes
½-cup melted butter
½-cup brown sugar, packed
½-cup Kentucky Bourbon
½-teaspoon salt
¼-teaspoon cinnamon
¼-teaspoon nutmeg
⅓-cup orange juice

Cook sweet potatoes 20 to 25-minutes in boiling water until tender with the touch of a fork. Drain and cool. Peel and mash. Add the remaining ingredients. Pour sweet potato mixture in greased baking dish. Bake 40-minutes at 375-degrees.

Candied Tomatoes
Preheat oven at 350-degrees.
Spray 9-x 13 x 2-inch casserole dish with vegetable cooking spray.

1-quart tomatoes
1 & ¼-scant cup brown sugar
½-stick butter
1-small onion, chopped
½-teaspoon salt
Pepper to taste

1-teaspoon vinegar

6 to 8-biscuits, split and toasted

    Line the bottom and sides of the prepared casserole dish with toasted biscuits. In a large saucepan, melt butter or margarine. Add tomatoes, brown sugar, chopped onion, salt, pepper, and vinegar. Heat and pour over biscuits. Bake 1-hour at 350-degrees. Serves 6 to 8.

Candied Sweet Potatoes
Preheat oven at 375-degrees.

Prepare greased baking pan.

6 to 8-medium sweet potatoes

1 & ½-cups brown sugar, firmly packed

½-cup granulated sugar

⅔-cup water

⅓-cup melted butter

½-teaspoon salt

⅓-teaspoon nutmeg

    Cook potatoes in boiling water until tender. Drain. Peel and cut in half, lengthwise. Place in greased baking pan, cut side up. Combine next 6-ingredients in a saucepan. Boil 6-minutes. Stir often. Pour over potatoes. Bake 30-minutes at 375-degrees. Baste during the baking.

Vegetable Quiche
Preheat at 350-degrees.

¼-cup mayonnaise

1-tablespoon flour

4-eggs, beaten

¼-cup milk

4-ounces Swiss cheese, grated

½-pound bacon, cooked and crumbled

1, 8-ounce package frozen mixed vegetables

1/8-teaspoon nutmeg
1-unbaked pie shell

     Cook vegetables 5-minutes and drain. Combine mayonnaise, flour, egg, and milk. Add cheese and vegetables. Pour into pie shell and bake 1-hour at 350-degrees. If not thoroughly set; bake another 15-minutes at 375-degrees.

Potatoes-in-Casserole
Preheat oven at 400-degrees.
Set out casserole dish.

4-pounds white potatoes
⅓-cup soft butter
3-teaspoons salt
2-eggs, slightly beaten
Hot milk

     Peel and cook potatoes until tender. Slightly mash either by electric mixer or by hand. Add seasonings and eggs. Beat until smooth. Add hot milk to suit your taste of consistency. Put mashed potatoes into casserole dish. Make a depression in the center of the mound. Fill center with the following mixture:

Filling:
1-cup coarsely shredded American cheese
3-egg yolks, beaten with fork
¼-cup melted butter, more if you like
1-tablespoon coffee cream
⅛-teaspoon cayenne pepper
¼-teaspoon dry mustard
¼-teaspoon salt

Mix ingredients together. Pour in center of mound. Sprinkle with paprika. Bake 30-minutes at 400-degrees or until lightly brown. This can be put together several hours in advance and baked 45-minutes.

Hash Brown Casserole

My sister, Mabel got this recipe – known as Funeral Potatoes - when she worked at Magnavox in the early 1950's making audio speakers.

Preheat oven at 350-degrees.

Set out 3-quart casserole dish or 9 x 13-inch Pyrex dish.

2-pounds frozen, diced hash brown potatoes
1-can cream of mushroom soup with ½-can milk
1-cup sour cream
1-cup grated cheddar cheese
¼-cup grated onion, sauté in 1-tablespoon butter
Salt and pepper to taste
3-tablespoons butter, melted
¾-cup Cornflake crumbs

Thaw the frozen potatoes. Place in casserole or Pyrex dish. Combine soup, milk, sour cream, cheese, onion, salt and pepper to taste. Mix well. Spread over potatoes. In a separate pan, melt butter and combine cornflakes. Sprinkle buttered flakes over casserole mixture. Bake uncovered for 30 to 45-minutes at 350-degrees or until hot and bubbly throughout.

Suggestion: If you want to use fresh potatoes, peel and dice 6 to 8- potatoes. Cook slightly before placing in casserole dish.

Corn Pudding

Preheat oven at 350-degrees.
Set out baking dish.

2-tablespoons margarine
3-eggs

3-tablespoons sugar
1-tablespoon salt
½-teaspoon baking powder
1, 2 & ½-ounce can cream style corn

    Melt margarine in baking dish. Beat eggs and sugar together in small bowl. Mix flour, salt, baking powder, and corn in a medium size bowl. Add milk to egg mixture and beat. Add melted margarine. Stir well. Pour mixture back into baking dish. Bake 40 to 50-minutes at 350-degrees or until pudding is set in the middle.

Broccoli Casserole
Preheat oven at 400-degrees.
Prepare buttered casserole dish.

1-package frozen chopped broccoli, do not add water
½-can cream of mushroom soup
½-cup grated sharp cheese
½-cup mayonnaise, not salad dressing
1-tablespoon grated onion
2-eggs, well beaten
½-cup cheese cracker crumbs, like Cheese-Its

    Cook broccoli according to package directions. Drain well. Combine all ingredients, except cracker crumbs. Blend with cooked broccoli. Pour into buttered casserole dish. Sprinkle cracker crumbs on top. Bake for 20- minutes at 400-degrees. Serves 4 to 5.

Sweet Potato Soufflé
Preheat oven at 400-degrees.
Set out shallow baking dish.

4-cups mashed sweet potatoes
¾-stick margarine
1-cup sugar
1-cup milk

Mix ingredients above and pour into a shallow baking dish.

Topping:
1-cup brown sugar
2-cups crushed cornflakes
½-cup nuts

Mix brown sugar, cornflakes, and nuts. Spread on top of sweet potato mixture. Bake 30-minutes at 400-degrees.

Squash Casserole
Preheat oven at 450-degrees.
Set out baking dish.

3-pounds small yellow squash, about 6-cups
¼-cup butter
1 & ½-cups chopped onions
½-cup milk
2-large eggs
1-cup grated cheese
½-cup cracker crumbs
Salt and pepper
Melted butter

Wash squash. Do not peel. Cut into small pieces. Cook in salted water until tender. Do not overcook. Drain well. Pour into baking dish. Add butter, salt, pepper, and onion. Combine milk, cheese, and eggs. Mix well with squash. Sweeten to taste. Top with a little melted butter and cracker crumbs. Bake 20-minutes at 450-degrees.

Squash Casserole II
Preheat oven at 350-degrees.
Lightly grease 12-x 7 x 2-inch Pyrex dish.
1-pound small to medium yellow squash, cut into ¼-inch slices

1-pound small to medium zucchini, cut into ¼-inch slices
½-cup water
½-teaspoon salt
1-cup onion, finely chopped
1-cup red bell pepper, chopped
½-cup butter
1-egg, beaten
4-ounces cheddar cheese, shredded
1, 8-ounce can sliced water chestnuts, drained
⅔-cup mayonnaise
2 teaspoons sugar
¼-teaspoon black pepper

    Combine yellow and zucchini squash, water, and salt in a saucepan. Bring to boil. Cover and simmer 10-minutes or until squash is fork tender. Drain and set aside. Sauté red peppers and onion in butter for about 3- minutes. Combine with vegetables and remaining ingredients. Spoon into greased dish. Bake 30-minutes at 350-degrees or until bubbly.

Old-Fashioned Rice Pudding
Preheat oven at 300-degrees.
Set out flat baking dish.

¼-cup sugar
⅓-cup uncooked rice
4-cups milk, scalded
½-teaspoon salt
2-tablespoons butter
2-tablespoons vanilla

    Combine all ingredients in a flat baking dish and place in a slow 300-degree oven. Bake 1 & ½-hours or until rice is tender and pudding is thick and creamy, but not dry. Stir every 15-minutes with a fork, carefully turning under the browned topping and scrapping the edges of the pan. Serve hot or cold. Yield: 5 servings.

French-Fried Onion Rings

2-large onions, peeled
1-cup evaporated milk
Flour
Hot oil

Slice onions ¼-inch thick. Separate into rings. Dip in flour. Dip in evaporated milk. Dip in flour again. Drop into deep, hot fat at 375-degrees and fry until golden brown, about 2 to 3-minutes. Drain on paper towels. Sprinkle with salt. Serve hot.

Cabbage

My sweet Bessie gave me this recipe when I was newly married.

Preheat oven at 350-degrees.
Set out 1 & ½-quart casserole dish.

1-medium head cabbage
½-cup salted boiling water
3-tablespoons butter
3-tablespoons flour
½-teaspoon salt
1 & ½-cups milk
¼-cup plain breadcrumbs

Finely shred cabbage. Cook in boiling water for 8-9 minutes. Drain well. Place in casserole. Melt butter, stir in flour and salt until smooth. Add milk gradually. Stir until it thickens. Pour over cabbage. Sprinkle breadcrumbs on top. Dot with butter. Bake for 20 to 25-minutes at 350-degrees.

Sweet Potato Casserole
Aunt Lucy's recipe,
Moultrie, Georgia

Preheat oven at 350-degrees.

Prepare buttered casserole dish.

2-medium sweet potatoes

1, #2-size can crushed pineapple

½-cup chopped pecans

½ package golden raisins

    Grate sweet potatoes. In a large bowl, combine other ingredients. Add 1-cup milk and 2-teaspoons sugar. Pour into buttered casserole dish. Dot with butter on top. Bake 1-hour at 350-degrees.

Vern's Ratatouille

3-medium red or yellow bell peppers, chopped

3 to 4-onions, chopped

4-medium eggplants, peeled and cubed

4 to 5-summer or zucchini squash

3-stalks celery, sliced

12-fresh mushrooms

¼ to ½-teaspoon garlic salt

1-teaspoon basil, fresh or freeze-dried

Salt and pepper to taste

1, 28-ounce can crushed tomatoes with puree

1, 10-ounce can Ro-Tel tomatoes with green chilies

    Sauté bell peppers and onions in about 3-tablespoons oil. Add crushed tomatoes and tomatoes with chilies. Bring to a boil. Add the rest of the vegetables. Return to boil, reduce heat, and simmer for about 45-minutes. Stir often. Vegetables will become tender and thick. Do not add water.

Spinach-Cheese Pie

Preheat oven at 325-degrees.

Lightly grease 10-inch pie pan.

2-boxes frozen chopped spinach, thawed and squeezed very dry

¾ to 1-pound part skim Ricotta cheese

2-eggs

2, 6-ounce packages Muenster cheese

Salt and pepper

Onion powder

Line pie pan with 1-package Muenster cheese. Mix together other ingredients and pour into pie pan. Bake 20-minutes at 325-degrees. Remove from oven and place the other package of Muenster cheese over top. Bake another 20-minutes at 325-degrees. Cool ½-hour before slicing.

French Green Bean Casserole

From my friend, Tuc McCoy.

Preheat oven at 350-degrees.

Set out baking dish.

2-cans French-cut green beans, drained

2-cans shoe-peg corn, drained

1-cup crushed Ritz crackers

1-cup sour cream

1-cup grated cheese

2-cans cream of celery soup

½-cup melted butter

½-cup almonds

Place green beans and corn in a baking dish. Top with sour cream, grated cheese and cream of celery soup. Mix well. Top with cracker crumbs, melted butter, and almonds. Bake at 350-degrees until bubbly.

ENTREES

Hot Chicken Salad
Served at Grace Episcopal Church bazaar luncheon at Thanksgiving.
Preheat oven at 350-degrees.
Prepare buttered 9 x 13 x 2-inch Pyrex dish.

5-cups cooked chicken (4 to 5- pound hen), cubed
3-hard-boiled eggs, chopped
3-tablespoons minced onion
2, 8-ounce cans water chestnuts, drained and sliced
1-cup Hellmann's Mayonnaise
1-can cream of mushroom soup
1-can cream of chicken soup
½-cup buttered breadcrumbs
¾-cup sliced almonds, toasted
1-large jar sliced mushrooms, drained

Mix together chicken, eggs, onion, water chestnuts, mayonnaise, and soups. Place in buttered dish. Sprinkle with buttered breadcrumbs. Bake for 20-minutes at 350-degrees. Sprinkle with toasted almonds. Bake about 10-more minutes.

This dish can be prepared in advance and refrigerated overnight. However, do not put on breadcrumbs or almonds until you bake the dish. Before you bake it, remove from refrigerator for 30-minutes. We served this dish with green beans, cranberry salad, and rolls.

Working Girl Chicken
Preheat oven at 350-degrees.
Set out Dutch oven or roaster.

1-whole chicken, cut up
1-can cream of mushroom soup, do not add water
1-lemon, thinly sliced

½ to ¾ of 1, 8-ounce carton sour cream
Capers
Mushrooms, sliced

    Lightly brown chicken and place in a Dutch oven or roaster. Top chicken with lemon slices and sprinkle freely with capers. Add mushrooms and spoon on mushroom soup. Bake chicken for 45 to 50-minutes at 350-degrees. Remove chicken and place on a platter. Add sour cream to gravy in roaster. Mix thoroughly. Place chicken back into roaster and coat with mixture. Serve over rice.

Beef Macaroni Loaf

Preheat oven at 350-degrees.
Grease 9 x 5 x 3-inch loaf pan.
Line the bottom with double thick strips of foil.
Grease foil. Leave 1-inch over-hang.

Macaroni layer:

1, 8-ounce package elbow macaroni
2-tablespoons butter or margarine
2-tablespoons flour
1-teaspoon salt
¼-teaspoon black pepper
1-egg
2-cups milk
½-cup Parmesan cheese, grated

Meat layer:

¼-cup onion, chopped
1-tablespoon butter
1 & ½-pounds ground beef
1-egg
1-can condensed tomato soup

1-teaspoon salt
1-teaspoon black pepper

Sauce:

1, 8-ounce can tomato sauce
1-teaspoon sugar
¼-teaspoon basil (can use freeze dried, tastes fresh)

Cook macaroni according to directions. Drain and return to kettle. Stir in butter. Sprinkle over flour, salt, and pepper. Toss and mix well. Place cooked macaroni in prepared loaf pan. Beat egg, stir in milk and pour over macaroni mixture. Cook over medium heat, stirring constantly until thickened. Remove from heat and stir in Parmesan cheese.

Sauté onion in butter until soft. Add ground beef. Brown and break up meat with fork as it cooks. Beat and add egg. Stir in ½-can of tomato soup, salt and pepper. Stir into cooked mixture.

Spoon ½-macaroni mixture in even layers in prepared pan. Top with all of meat mixture. Add remaining macaroni mixture. Bake at 350-degrees for 1-hour, or until brown and firm. Make sauce while loaf bakes. Heat tomato sauce with remaining tomato soup, sugar, and basil to boiling. Simmer 3-minutes to blend flavors.

Cook loaf in pan 10-minutes. Loosen sides with knife. Then lift up ends of foil and set loaf on a heated serving platter. Slide out foil. Serve sauce separately. Spoon sauce over separate servings.

Elizabeth's Roast Beef
Preheat oven at 300 to 350- degrees.
Set out roasting pan.

3 to 5-pound roast
3-teaspoons olive oil
2 to 3-teaspoons wine vinegar
1 or 2- bay leaves

Dash of thyme

1-small onion

2-beef bouillon cubes

1-teaspoon Worcestershire Sauce

½ to 1-cup water

 Prepare roast with salt and pepper. Make marinade by adding together all other ingredients. Boil for 5-minutes then pour over roast. Marinate in refrigerator for 24-hours. Turn roast frequently. Cook with juices in oven, basting occasionally until done.

Stuffed Meatloaf

Preheat oven at 350-degrees.

Grease 8-inch baking pan.

1-pound ground sirloin

1-cup Quaker Quick oats

1, 15 & ½-ounce jar Marinara sauce

½-cup chopped onion

⅓-cup Parmesan cheese, grated

1-egg

1-tablespoon Worcestershire Sauce

⅓-cup zucchini, shredded

½-cup Mozzarella cheese, shredded

Sliced black olives

 Combine beef, oats, ½-cup spaghetti, onion, Parmesan cheese, egg, Worcestershire Sauce, and pepper. Mix well. Separate mixture into 2-equal parts. Shape each into a patty about 7-inches in diameter. Place shredded zucchini on one patty within ½-inch of edge. Top with the other patty. Pinch sides together to hold the zucchini. Smooth edges into a rounded loaf. Top loaf with 1-cup spaghetti sauce and Mozzarella cheese. Garnish with black olives. Serve with remaining sauce.

Brisket

I got this recipe from a TV show. It's the best I have ever made.

Preheat oven at 500-degrees.

Set out a roaster.

6-pound brisket
4-cloves garlic
2-onions, sliced
1-cup ketchup
1-cup water
Paprika

Make slits in the brisket and insert 4-or more-garlic cloves. Place brisket flesh side up in 500-degree oven. Roast 30-minutes. Turn over to fat side and roast another 25-minutes. Remove from oven. Reduce heat to 350-degrees. Place 2-onions, sliced and separated, under the meat. Cover brisket with lots of paprika and ketchup. Then, pour 1-cup of water around the side of pan. Bake 45-minutes to 1-hour, checking from time to time to see if you need to add more water. Take brisket out of roaster. Cool. Cut cross grain. Serve with potato cake made with zucchini and shredded Idaho potatoes and applesauce on the side.

Make gravy:

Add 2 to-3 tablespoons flour to a cup of milk. Cook until thickens, stirring constantly. I use Gold Medal Wonder flour. It mixes quickly and does not clump.

Tortilla Pie

From my niece Connie Martin.

Preheat oven at 400-degrees.

Set out round 2-quart casserole dish.

1-pound ground beef
1-medium onion, chopped
1-clove garlic, minced

1-tablespoon butter or margarine

1, 8-ounce can enchilada sauce

1-tablespoon chili powder

1-teaspoon salt

¼-teaspoon pepper

6-corn tortillas

2-cups shredded Longhorn Cheddar cheese

½-cup water

    Brown beef, onion, and garlic in butter. Drain. Add sauce, chili powder, salt, and pepper. In a round 2-quart casserole alternate layers of tortillas with meat sauce and 1 & ½-cups cheese. Sprinkle remaining ½-cup cheese over top. Pour the water at the edge of casserole to the bottom. Cover and bake for 25-minutes at 400-degrees. Uncover and let stand 5-minutes before serving.

Meatballs with Cabbage

1-can tomato soup

1-pound ground beef

1-cup cooked rice

2-small onions, chopped

¼-cup milk

1-egg

1-tablespoon butter or shortening

1-medium head of cabbage

Salt and pepper to taste

    Parboil cabbage. Cool. Mix ground beef, chopped onions, pepper and salt together and add unbeaten egg. Blend thoroughly. Roll into small balls about the size of golf balls. Separate leaves of cabbage. Enclose each meatball with 2 or 3-leaves. Brown in butter or shortening. Leave in same cooking pan and cover with tomato soup. Simmer slowly for

1-hour on top of the burner. Baste frequently, turning each meatball several times.

Chile Relleno Bake

Preheat oven at 325-degrees.

Set out 8 x 8-inch casserole dish.

1 & ½-cups Jack cheese, shredded
1 & ½-cups cheddar cheese, shredded
2, 4 to 5-ounce cans whole green chilies, drained
1-large can evaporated milk
3-eggs, beaten

Combine cheeses. Spread half on the bottom of pan. Split chilies and place over cheese. Top with remaining cheese. Gradually add milk to flour and blend well. Add eggs, blend well. Pour over casserole. Cover with foil and bake 45-minutes at 325-degrees. Cool 10-minutes and cut into squares.

Chile Relleno Bake II

Preheat oven at 325-degrees.

Set out casserole dish.

2, 4-ounce cans whole chilies
10-ounces sharp cheddar cheese, grated
1-pound ground round beef
1-medium onion, chopped
4-whole eggs
1 & ½-cups whole milk
½-cup flour
Several dashes Tabasco Sauce
Salt and pepper to taste

Place 1-can whole chilies in bottom of casserole dish, do not grease. Add ½ of the grated cheese. Cook beef and chopped onion until beef is no longer pink. Pour over chilies and cheese. Top with remaining cheese and chilies. Beat together eggs, milk, flour, and Tabasco. Pour over casserole mixture. Bake 40 to 60-minutes at 325-degrees. Dip off excess grease.

Hamburger Stroganoff

½-cup minced onion
1-clove garlic, minced
¼-cup butter
1-pound ground beef
2-tablespoons flour
1-teaspoon salt
¼-teaspoon pepper
1-pound fresh mushrooms, or 1, 8-ounce can sliced mushrooms
1, 10 & ½-ounce can cream of chicken soup, undiluted
1-cup sour cream
2-tablespoons parsley, minced

    Sauté onion and garlic in butter over medium heat. Add meat and cook until brown. Add flour, salt, pepper, and mushrooms. Cook 5-minutes. Add soup and simmer uncovered 10-minutes. Stir in sour cream and heat through. Sprinkle with parsley. Serve with egg noodles.

Texas Chili
From a dear friend from Texas, Mabel Wilson.

1-tablespoon oil or fat
2-pounds ground round or sirloin
1-medium onion, chopped
4-tablespoons chili powder
1-tablespoon paprika
1-tablespoon Worcestershire Sauce
1-teaspoon soy sauce
1-teaspoon salt

Pepper to taste
¼-teaspoon sweet basil
¼-teaspoon cumin
2, 8-ounce cans tomato sauce, or 1, 16-ounce can
2, 8-ounce cans water, or 1, 16-ounce can
2-cans plain pinto beans, rinsed and drained
Fresh tomato, chopped
Lettuce, shredded

     Sauté onion in oil or fat. Cook until clear, not brown. Add ground beef and cook until no longer pink. Add chili powder, Worcestershire Sauce, basil, cumin, tomato sauce, and water. Mix well and simmer 15-minutes. Add pinto beans. Cook 20-minutes. Serve over corn chips. Top with grated cheese, chopped onion, tomato and lettuce. Finish with salsa over all, if desired.

Vegetable Soup with Meatballs
First, make your favorite vegetable soup.

1-pound ground turkey or beef
1-egg
½-cup small onion, finely chopped
¼-cup Italian breadcrumbs
¼-cup milk
1-teaspoon salt
¼-teaspoon pepper

     Mix all ingredients and shape into meatballs 1-inch in diameter. Drop meatballs into vegetable soup during the last 20-minutes of cooking.

Meat Loaf
Preheat oven at 400-degrees.
Set out round or loaf pans.

2 & ½-pounds ground beef

1 & ¼- pounds ground pork or veal
2-slices bread, crumbled
⅓-cup quick cooking oatmeal
4-eggs, beaten
2-teaspoons salt
Pepper to taste
1-tablespoon Dijon Mustard
1-cup tomato sauce
1-medium onion, chopped
1-small can evaporated milk

 Mix all ingredients well. Chill and place in pans. Bake for 1-hour at 400-degrees. You could freeze one to serve later.

Sauce:

1-cup tomato sauce
½-cup milk
4-tablespoons brown sugar
4-tablespoons mustard
4-tablespoons vinegar

 Heat thoroughly. Serve over meat loaf.

Meat Loaf II

Preheat at 350-degrees.
Set out 8 x 4-inch loaf or broiler pan.

¾-cup ketchup, divided
½-cup quick cooking oatmeal
¼-cup fresh onions, minced
2-tablespoons fresh parsley, chopped
1-teaspoon brown sugar
¼-teaspoon salt
¼-teaspoon pepper

2-large egg whites, lightly beaten
1 & ½-pound ground round

    Combine ½-cup ketchup, oats, and the next 6-ingredients in a large bowl. Add meat and stir until just blended. Shape meat mixture into loaf pan or on a broiler, coated with cooking spray. Brush ¼-cup ketchup over meat loaf. Bake for 1-hour and 10-minutes at 350-degrees. Let stand 10-minutes before slicing. Yield: 6 servings.

Mini Pork Meat Loaves
*I made these for the women of the church luncheons
at St. Andrew's Episcopal Church.*
Preheat oven at 350-degrees.
Set out baking pan.

3-tablespoons chutney
1-egg, beaten
¼-cup breadcrumbs
2-tablespoons raisins
1-tablespoon dried, minced onion
1-teaspoon prepared mustard
½-teaspoon salt
⅛-teaspoon pepper
1-pound ground pork

    Snip chutney into small pieces and set aside. In a medium bowl, combine egg and chutney. Stir in breadcrumbs, raisins, onions, mustard, salt, and pepper. Add ground pork and mix well. Shape into 4, 4 x 2-inch loaves. Bake 35 to 40-minutes at 350-degrees or until meat is done. With this dish, I serve green beans, potato salad on lettuce leaves, rolls, and lemon pie for dessert.

Country Ham & Redeye Gravy

2-slices, ¼-inch thick uncooked hickory-smoked country ham

2-tablespoons vegetable oil

1-cup strong coffee

2-tablespoons all purpose flour

½-teaspoon paprika

Cut gashes into fat to keep ham from curling. Sauté ham in a cast iron skillet over low heat for 3-4 minutes on each side. Remove ham from skillet and keep warm. Combine coffee and flour and add to pan drippings, stirring constantly until thickened. Add paprika. Serve over ham. Yield: 2 servings.

Aunt Jenny's Hamburger Balls

Preheat oven at 450-degrees.

Set out skillet with cover.

1-pound ground beef

2-tablespoons onion, finely chopped

2-tablespoons green pepper, chopped

¼-cup cornmeal

1-teaspoon chili powder

1 & ½-teaspoon dry mustard

1-teaspoon salt

⅛-teaspoon pepper

½-cup milk

1-egg

¼-cup flour

¼-cup shortening

1 & ½-cups canned tomatoes

Combine hamburger, onions, green peppers, cornmeal, seasonings, milk, and egg. Blend thoroughly. Form 12-balls and roll in flour. Brown in hot shortening in skillet. Add remaining flour and tomatoes. Cover and bake for 30 to 45-minutes at 450-degrees. Serves 6.

For an oven dinner, place 6-quartered potatoes, 6-halved carrots, and 6-whole small onions. Place vegetables and meatballs together and bake in hot oven.

Turkey Breast with Orange Glaze
Preheat oven at 325-degrees.
Set out 13 x 9 x 2-inch pan.

5-pound turkey breast, skinned and boned
1-cup orange juice
1-teaspoon grated orange rind
1-teaspoon rubbed sage
½-teaspoon dried whole thyme
½-teaspoon pepper
1-tablespoon cornstarch
¼-cup water
2-cups fresh or frozen raspberries, thawed
⅓-cup sugar

Place turkey breast in pan. Pour orange juice over breast and sprinkle with orange rind, sage, thyme, and pepper. Cover and bake 1 & ½- hours at 325-degrees or until meat thermometer registers 170-degrees. Baste frequently with pan drippings. Transfer turkey to serving platter. Measure 1-cup pan drippings. Add water if necessary to obtain 1-cup. Strain and set aside. Combine cornstarch and water in a saucepan, stirring well. Add raspberries, sugar, and reserved pan drippings. Cook over medium heat until sauce thickens, stirring frequently. Serve with turkey. Yield: 8-10 servings.

Country Captain Chicken

A great American recipe in the Southern tradition.

Preheat oven at 275-degrees.

Set out covered roasting pan.

2-fryers, cut up

1-bunch parsley

4-green peppers

2-large onions

Cooking oil

1, #2 & ½-size can tomatoes

1-teaspoon mace

2-teaspoons curry powder

Salt and pepper to taste

1 clove garlic, chopped

Paprika

Flour

½-box currants

Cooked rice

½-pound blanched almonds, toasted

Fry chopped parsley, green peppers, and onions slowly in oil for 15-minutes. Put this mixture in a roaster. Add tomatoes, spices, salt, and pepper. Simmer 15-minutes. Add chopped garlic. Dredge chicken in a mixture of flour, salt, pepper, and paprika. Fry until golden brown. Place chicken in the sauce and simmer at 275-degrees in a covered roaster for 1 & ½-to 2-hours. Add currants ½-hour before serving. Arrange rice on a platter. Pour over sauce, and then place pieces of chicken on top. Sprinkle with toasted almonds and serve.

Tahiti Chicken
This is an old recipe from Kraft Foods.
Preheat oven at 350-degrees.
Set out baking dish.

1-broiler, cut up
¼-cup flour
¼-teaspoon salt
Dash of pepper
¼-cup margarine
1, 8-ounce bottle sweet and sour sauce dressing
½-cup pineapple tidbits, drained

Coat chicken with seasoned flour. Brown in margarine. Place in baking dish. Add sauce and pineapple tidbits. Cover and bake for 45-minutes at 350-degrees or until chicken is tender. Great served with rice.

Baked Chicken & Noodles
Set out kettle for stewing chicken, a saucepan,
and greased casserole dish.

5-pound stewing chicken
1-stalk celery
1-carrot
1-large onion
2-bay leaves
¼-cup chicken fat
2-tablespoons flour
3-cups chicken stock
2-egg yolks
½-cup cream
Salt and pepper
1, 8-ounce package noodles

Put whole chicken in a kettle with enough water to half cover. Toss in celery, carrot, onion, and bay leaves. Bring to a boil. Cover and reduce heat. Cook gently for about 2 & ½-hours or until chicken is very tender. Let the chicken rest in the stock until cool enough to handle. Then, remove and skim all fat from surface of stock. Scoop out seasoning vegetables and toss away. Save fat and stock to use later on. Remove chicken skin and discard. Pull meat off bones and cut into chunks.

Heat ¼-cup chicken fat in a saucepan. Smoothly stir in flour. Pour in chicken stock and cook, stirring constantly until sauce bubbles. Mix egg yolks and cream together in a bowl. Then, stir in the hot stock sauce a dribble at a time. Cook over low heat for about 5-minutes, stirring constantly. Season with salt and pepper.

Cook noodles until tender according to package directions. Drain. Start oven at 400-degrees. Grease a large casserole dish. Arrange alternate layers of noodles and chicken. Pour sauce over top and bake 20 to 25-minutes or until top is brown and bubbly. Yield: 8 servings.

Chicken Broccoli Casserole

We made this dish for luncheons at Grace Episcopal Church.

Preheat oven at 350-degrees.

Grease a 2-quart baking dish.

3-large double chicken breasts
2-packages of 16-ounce frozen broccoli florets
2-cans cream of chicken soup
1-cup mayonnaise
1-teaspoon lemon juice
½-teaspoon curry powder
8-ounces cheddar cheese, cut into cubes
1-cup buttered breadcrumbs
½-cup melted butter
Onion slice
Piece of celery

Cook chicken in salted water with onion and celery. Cool. Remove from bone and break into pieces. Cook broccoli in salted water for 5-minutes. Arrange broccoli over bottom of greased dish. Top with chicken. Mix other ingredients and pour over cubed cheese. Sprinkle with breadcrumbs buttered in ½-cup melted butter. Bake 30 to 45-minutes at 350-degrees.

Chicken Chow Mein

My sister-in-law, Thelma made this many times for me when I walked from school to her house for lunch.

2-cups chopped cooked chicken
2-tablespoons melted butter
2-cups celery, thinly sliced
2-cups chicken broth
1-teaspoon salt
Pepper to taste
1, 4-ounce can sliced mushrooms, drained
1, 16-ounce can mixed Chinese vegetables, drained
2-tablespoons cornstarch
3-tablespoons soy sauce

Lightly brown chicken in butter. Add celery, onion, pepper, salt, and chicken broth. Cook covered 5 to 10-minutes or until celery is tender. Add Chinese vegetables and mushrooms. Simmer 2-minutes. Dissolve cornstarch in soy sauce. Stir constantly until slightly thickened. Add to mixture. Serve over hot rice.

Chicken or Shrimp with Curry

3-tablespoons butter
1 & ½-teaspoons curry powder
½-medium onion, chopped
1-stalk celery, chopped

1 & ½-cups water
2-tablespoons flour
½-teaspoon salt
1-small can crushed pineapple
2-cups cooked chicken or shrimp
Chutney

    Melt butter and add curry powder. Stir and heat gently 1-minute. Add onion, celery, and water. Cook until celery and onion are tender. Add flour and salt. Stir well and bring to a boil. Add pineapple and ginger, if desired. Add chicken or shrimp and salt and pepper to taste. Simmer 10-minutes. Serve over rice with chutney on this side. To make this dish hot, add cayenne pepper.

Sour Cream Chicken
Preheat oven at 275-degrees.
Grease a 9 x 13 x 2-inch baking dish.

8-large chicken breasts, boned
8-slices bacon
1, 4-ounce jar dried chipped beef
1-can cream of mushroom soup
½-pint sour cream

    Wrap each chicken breast with a slice of bacon. Line the greased baking dish with beef. Place chicken breast over beef. Combine soup and sour cream and pour over chicken. Refrigerate. When ready to serve, bake uncovered for 2 to 3-hours at 275-degrees.

Sausage Dressing
Preheat oven at 350-degrees.
Set out 9 x 13 x 2-inch baking dish.

½-pound pork sausage, uncooked
1-small onion, diced

4-stalks celery, diced with a few leaves, finely chopped
5-cups corn bread
5 to 6-slices white bread, cubed and toasted
½-stack of saltine crackers, dampened and crushed
¼-teaspoon black pepper
3 & ½ to 4-cups chicken or turkey broth
2-eggs, beaten

     Cook onion and celery over medium heat in 2 to 3-tablespoons butter until tender. Cool slightly. Place in a large bowl. Add remaining ingredients with sausage. Stir well. Spoon dressing into baking dish. Bake 30-minutes at 350-degrees or until thoroughly heated. Yield: 8-10 servings.

SEAFOOD

Scalloped Oysters
Preheat oven at 350-degrees.
Set out 2-quart casserole dish.

1-quart fresh oysters, drain and reserve ½-cup oyster liquor
2 & ½-sleeves buttery crackers, crushed
½-teaspoon salt
½-teaspoon pepper
1-cup butter, melted
1 & ½-cups half & half cream
1-egg, beaten

Place cracker crumbs in a large bowl. Sprinkle with salt. Dribble butter over crumbs. Toss to combine. Mix ½-cup oyster liquor with half & half and beaten egg. Put ⅓ of crumbs over bottom of 2-quart casserole dish. Top with half of oysters and sprinkle with pepper. Pour half of cream mixture over oysters. Repeat layers. Finish with crumbs on top. Cover and chill overnight. Remove 30-minutes before baking. Bake at 350-degrees for 30-minutes.

Crab Soufflé
Preheat oven at 325-degrees.
Set out 1 & ½-quart casserole dish.

½-cup evaporated milk
1-cup shredded sharp cheddar cheese
½-teaspoon salt
Dash of black pepper
6-eggs, separated
1-cup crab meat, flaked

Heat milk in a double boiler. Add cheddar cheese, salt, and pepper. Remove from heat. Cool. Add beaten egg yolks. Fold in stiffly beaten egg whites. Place crabmeat in casserole dish. Top with mixture. Bake at 325- degrees for 45-minutes.

Tuna Loaf

2-cups flaked tuna
1-tablespoon vinegar
2-tablespoons ketchup
1-cup water
3-hard boiled eggs, chopped
12-stuffed olives with pimento, sliced
1-cup salad dressing
2-tablespoons gelatin

Soak gelatin in ½-cup cold water for 5-minutes. Pour on ½-cup boiling water. Mix tuna, vinegar, ketchup, and add eggs and olives. Mix gelatin with salad dressing. Add fish mixture. Place in mold and chill.

Tuna Artichoke Casserole

Preheat oven at 350-degrees.
Prepare buttered casserole dish.

1-can albacore tuna
1, 8-ounce can artichokes
1-small can mushrooms

Place artichokes in a buttered casserole dish. Drain tuna and flake over artichokes. Make a medium white sauce. Pour over ingredients. Top with butter. Sprinkle with Parmesan cheese. Bake 20 to 30-minutes at 350- degrees.

Salmon Patties

1, 15- to 16-ounce can pink salmon
1-egg
⅓-cup minced onion

½-cup flour
1 & ½-teaspoons baking powder
1 & ½-cups Crisco

    Drain salmon. Set aside 2-tablespoons of the salmon liquid. In a medium bowl, mix salmon, egg, and onion until sticky. Stir in flour. Add baking powder to salmon liquid. Stir into salmon mixture. Form into small patties. Fry in hot Crisco until golden brown, about 5-minutes. Serve with tartar sauce. Yield: 4 - 6 servings.

Sauté Shrimp

½-pound shrimp, peel, de-vein, and leave tails on
½-teaspoon freeze-dried basil
½-teaspoon freeze-dried parsley
½-teaspoon Italian seasoning
¼-teaspoon garlic salt
3 to 4-drops Frank's Red Hot Sauce
½-stick butter
2-tablespoons olive oil

    Melt butter in a sauté pan. Add olive oil. Blend in basil, parsley, Italian seasonings and Frank's Red Hot Sauce. Add shrimp. Cook until shrimp are pink, 2 to 3-minutes. Serve with your favorite crusty bread for dipping in the sauce.

BREADS

Cottage Cheese Raisin Loaf
From Fran Cicansky,
Regina, Saskatchewan, Canada

Preheat oven at 375-degrees.
Prepare greased loaf pan.

¼-cup butter
½-cup sugar
2-eggs
1-cup creamed cottage cheese
¾-cup raisins
2-cups flour
4-tablespoons baking powder
½-teaspoon soda
½-teaspoon cinnamon
¼-teaspoon salt
½-cup plus 2-tablespoons milk

    Beat butter and sugar until fluffy. Beat in eggs, cottage cheese, and raisins. Stir in flour mixed with baking powder, cinnamon, soda, and salt alternately with milk. Turn into greased loaf pan. Bake at 375-degrees for 10-minutes. Reduce heat to 350-degrees. Bake for 60-minutes or until a toothpick inserted in the center comes out dry. Cool in the pan 30-minutes. Invert pan and cool. Delicious when toasted.

Cranberry Nut Bread
Preheat oven at 350-degrees.
Grease and flour two 9-x 5-inch loaf pans.

4-cups all purpose flour
2-cups sugar
1-tablespoon baking powder

½-cup shortening

2-eggs

1 & ¾-cups orange juice

2-tablespoons fresh or frozen cranberries, coarsely chopped

1-cup walnuts, chopped

Grated orange peel

    Mix first 5-ingredients in a large bowl. With pastry blender, cut in shortening until mixture resembles coarse crumbs. In a medium bowl, beat eggs, orange juice, and grated orange peel with fork or whisk until blended. Stir in flour mixture until flour is just moistened. Gently stir in cranberries and walnuts into batter. Spoon batter evenly into loaf pans. Bake 55-minutes or until a toothpick inserted in the center comes out clean. Cool bread in pans on wire rack for 10-minutes. Remove from pans. Cool bread completely on rack. Makes 2, 1 & ½-pound loaves.

Hickory Nut Bread

Preheat oven at 350-degrees.

Prepared greased loaf pan.

3-cups all purpose flour, sifted before measuring

1-egg

1 & ½-teaspoon salt

5-tablespoons baking powder

¼-cup shortening

1 & ¼-cup milk

1-cup hickory nuts (or pecans)

    Sift flour, sugar, salt, and baking powder into mixing bowl. Add shortening and mix with a pastry blender or fork until ingredients have appearance of coarse cornmeal. Add milk and slightly beaten egg. Add hickory nuts last. Pour into well-greased loaf pan. Bake at 350-degrees for 60 to 70-minutes. When baked, turn out on rack to cool.

Pumpkin Bread
From Louise Hockers, Grace Episcopal Church Cookbook.

Preheat oven at 350 degrees.

Grease and flour a 9 x 5 x 3-inch loaf pan.

1-cup cooked pumpkin
½-cup vegetable oil
2-eggs
⅓-cup water
1 & ⅓-cups flour
½-cup candied fruit
½-cup chopped pecans
1 & ¼-cups sugar
½-teaspoon salt
1-teaspoon soda
½-teaspoon cinnamon
½-teaspoon nutmeg

In a large bowl, stir together oil, eggs, water, and pumpkin. Sift together flour, salt, soda, sugar, and spices. Add dry ingredients to the first mixture. Beat until smooth. Add 1-tablespoon flour to the candied fruit and nuts before adding to the mixture. Pour into pans and bake 1-hour. Cover pans loosely with foil for the last 30-minutes of baking.

This makes great Christmas bread.

Cornbread

Preheat oven at 400-degrees.

Set out cast iron skillet.

1 & ½-cups sifted flour
3 & ½-teaspoons baking powder
1-teaspoon salt
⅓-cup Crisco, melted
1-egg, beaten well
1-cup milk

Sift flour with baking powder and salt. Add cornmeal and mix together. Melt Crisco in iron skillet. Combine beaten egg, milk, and melted Crisco. Add flour and blend. Pour into hot greased skillet and bake in hot oven, 400-degrees, for 25 to 30-minutes. If you like sweet cornbread, add 3-tablespoons sugar into the dry mixture.

Cornbread II

Preheat oven at 425-degrees.

Set out iron skillet.

1-cup cornmeal
½-cup all purpose flour
1-tablespoon baking powder
½-teaspoon baking soda
½-teaspoon salt
1-egg, beaten
1-cup buttermilk
¼-cup bacon drippings

Mix the first 5-ingredients. Mix well. Add egg and buttermilk and stir until smooth. Place drippings in cast iron skillet. Heat in oven at 425-degrees for 5-minutes. Remove skillet from oven and pour hot bacon drippings into batter and mix well. Quickly pour batter into skillet. Bake at 425-degrees for 20 to 25-minutes or until golden brown.

Hushpuppies

2-cups white cornmeal
1-egg
1-teaspoon baking powder
¼-teaspoon salt
1 & ½-cups whole milk
½-cup onion, finely chopped

Form into balls and cook in deep fat.

Kentucky Spoon Bread
Preheat oven at 400-degrees.
Prepare buttered deep-dish casserole.

½-cup cornmeal
2-cups whole milk
1-tablespoon butter
3-eggs, separated
½-teaspoon salt
½-teaspoon baking powder

Place milk in double boiler. Add cornmeal and stir until thick. Add butter, beaten egg yolks, baking powder, and salt. To this mixture, add stiffly beaten egg whites. Place in a buttered deep-dish casserole and bake at 400-degrees for 35-minutes. Serve immediately with more butter on each serving.

Pumpernickel Bread
From Gloria McElearney - July 1979.
Prepare greased baking sheets sprinkled with cornmeal.

3-packages yeast
1 & ½-cups lukewarm water
½-cup molasses
3-tablespoons caraway seeds
1-tablespoon salt
Rind of 1-orange, grated, or ½-teaspoon orange extract
2-tablespoons butter, softened
3-cups rye flour
3-cups all-purpose flour, sifted

Dissolve yeast with lukewarm water in a bowl. With a wooden spoon, stir in molasses, caraway seed, salt, orange rind (or extract), butter, and rye flour, and add enough all-purpose flour to make a soft dough.

With a wooden spoon, add 3-cups sifted all-purpose flour or enough to make soft dough. Turn onto a lightly floured pastry board. Knead dough 8 to 10-minutes or until smooth and elastic.

Place dough in a greased bowl. Turn over to coat entire surface. Cover with a damp cloth. Let rise in a warm place until dough doubles in bulk. This takes about 2-hours.

Punch dough down. Shape into 2-free form loaves or into approximately 24-rolls. Place on greased baking sheets sprinkled with cornmeal. Let rise about 45-minutes or until almost doubled in bulk. Meanwhile, preheat oven at 450-degrees. Brush tops of bread with water and place in oven. Bake loaves for 10-minutes at 450-degrees. Reduce heat to 350- degrees and bake 30-minutes longer. For rolls, bake at 375-degrees for 20-minutes.

For a nicely glazed crust, remove bread from oven 10-minutes before baking is completed. Brush with an egg white that has been lightly beaten with 1-tablespoon water. For an extra flavor, sprinkle at this time with coarse salt or caraway seeds. Cool loaves before slicing.

PIES

Meringues
Bake while you sleep....
Prepare a baking sheet with brown paper or parchment paper.
Preheat oven at 400-degrees.

6-egg whites
1 & ½-teaspoons lemon juice or ½-teaspoon cream of tartar
2-cups sugar

Beat egg whites with lemon juice or cream of tartar until frothy. Gradually beat in sugar a little at a time. Beat until stiff and glossy. Drop by small spoonfuls onto baking sheet, or heap into high mounds and hollow-out center with back of spoon. Place in oven. Close the door. Turn heat off. Do not peek! Let stand over night in oven. Makes 12-meringues. To serve, fill with ice cream, chocolate or butterscotch sauce, or fresh fruit.

Pastry Shell
Prepare 8 or 9-inch pie plate.
Preheat oven at 450-degrees.

1 & ½-cups all-purpose flour, sifted
½-teaspoon salt
½-cup shortening (Crisco)
3-tablespoons cold water

Combine flour and salt in a mixing bowl. Use a pastry blender or 2-knives in a scissor fashion and cut shortening into flour until it breaks into size of small peas. Blend ⅓-cup of this mixture with water. Blend this into flour mixture until dough holds together. Form pastry into a flat and round shape. Refrigerate ½-hour before rolling out on a lightly floured surface. Fit pastry into pie plate and make attractive edges. Prick the sides and bottom closely and deeply with a fork. Refrigerate ½-hour.

Bake at 450-degrees for 12 to 15-minutes or until golden. Peek after 5-minutes. If bubbles appear, prick with fork. Cool on wire rack before filling.

Wash Day Cobbler
Preheat oven at 375-degrees.

Melt 1-stick butter or margarine in a 9 x 13 x 2-inch glass dish. Pour fruit of your choice - 1-can of peach, apple, or cherry pie filling - over butter. Do not stir! Bake at 375-degrees for 35-minutes or until golden.

Nutmeg Sauce for Peach Cobbler
⅔-cup sugar

¼-teaspoon fresh nutmeg, grated

2-teaspoons cornstarch

Pinch of salt

1-cup boiling water

1, 3-inch piece orange peel, dried or fresh

2-tablespoons Brandy

Place sugar, nutmeg, cornstarch, and salt in a quart saucepan Stir well and pour in cup of boiling water stirring as you pour. Add orange peel and set over medium heat. Boil gently for 10-minutes. Set aside until ready serve. Reheat without boiling and add Brandy. Serve warm with peach cobbler. Note: take out the orange peel before serving.

Peach Dumplings
Preheat oven at 450-degrees.

Set out 8-inch layer pan.

2-cups sifted flour

3-teaspoons baking powder

1-teaspoon salt

¼-cup shortening

⅔ to ¾-cup milk

1 & ½-cups peaches, sliced

¼-cup sugar

½-teaspoon cinnamon

    Sift together flour, baking powder, and salt. Cut in shortening. Add milk to make soft dough. Turn out on lightly floured pastry cloth and knead gently for ½-minute. Roll out to rectangle 10 x 12-inch in size. Cover evenly with sliced peaches. Mix together sugar and cinnamon and sprinkle over peaches. Roll dough jelly roll style. Cut into ¼-inch slices. Place cut-side down around the edge of an 8-inch layer pan. Pour hot syrup over dumplings. Bake in 450-degree oven for about 25-minutes. Makes 8-dumplings.

Prepare syrup:

1-cup sugar

1-cup water or peach juice

    Put together in small saucepan. Heat to boiling point.

Cottage Cheese Pie

Preheat oven at 350-degrees.

Set out 9-inch unbaked pastry shell.

1 & ½-cups cottage cheese

2-tablespoons flour

1-tablespoon butter

½-cup sugar

2-tablespoons cream

3-eggs, separated

Pinch of salt

    Mix cottage cheese, flour, and cream together until smooth. Beat egg yolks lightly, add sugar and mix with cottage cheese. Add butter and salt. Beat egg whites until stiff and fold into mixture. Pour into 9-inch unbaked pastry shell. Bake at 350-degrees for 30-minutes or until firm. Serve hot or cold.

Ritz Cracker Pie
Preheat oven at 300-degrees.
Prepare greased 9 x 12-inch glass pan.

6-egg whites, beaten stiffly
2-cups sugar
1 & ½-cups pecans, chopped
40-Ritz Crackers, rolled and crushed finely
2-teaspoons vanilla
1-pint whipping cream
4-tablespoons Sherry
2-rounded tablespoons confectioners sugar

Beat eggs whites until stiff. Stir in sugar, cracker crumbs, nuts, and vanilla. Bake in greased 9 x 12-inch glass pan at 300-degrees for 45-minutes. Let cool. Add Sherry and confectioners sugar to whipped cream and spread immediately over top. Let stand in the refrigerator for 12 to 24-hours.

Cherry Cream Cheese Tarts
Preheat oven at 350-degrees.
Prepare muffin pan with paper liners.

2, 8-ounce packages cream cheese, softened
1-cup sugar
2-large eggs
1-teaspoon vanilla extract
12-Vanilla Wafers
1-can Cherry Pie Filling

Beat cream cheese with electric mixer at medium speed until light and fluffy. Gradually add sugar, mixing well after each additional portion.

Stir in vanilla. Place a Vanilla Wafer in each paper lined muffin pan cup. Spoon cream cheese mixture over wafers. Fill each cup full. Bake at 350-degrees for 20-minutes. Let cool in muffin pan. Cover and chill overnight. To serve, top each with a small amount of Cherry Pie Filling. Makes 12 servings.

Banana Split Pie

1, 13 x 9 x 2-inch glass baking dish.
2-cups Graham Cracker crumbs
½-cup melted butter
¼-cup sugar

Mix together and press into the bottom of baking dish. Chill 1 hour.

Prepare filling:

2-cups confectioners sugar, sifted
2-eggs
1-teapoon vanilla
1-cup butter

Cream together and spread over the crumb crust. Chill 1 hour.

Topping:

4 to 5-ripe bananas, sliced
2, 10-ounce packages frozen strawberries, drained
1, 16-ounce can crushed pineapples, drained
1-cup whipping cream, whipped
1-cup pecans, chopped
1, 4-ounce jar Maraschino Cherries, drained and chopped

Layer topping over the filling in the order listed. Cut into squares. Makes 12 to 15-servings. Keep refrigerated.

Kentucky Bourbon Apple Pie

Set out 9-inch deep-dish pan.

1-cup all-purpose flour
1-tablespoon sugar
¼-teaspoon salt
1, 3-ounce package cream cheese, cubed
¼-cup unsalted butter, cubed

Combine flour, sugar, and salt in a large bowl. With pastry blender, cut in cream cheese and butter until mixture resembles course crumbs. Knead pastry into a ball. Flatten slightly, cover and refrigerate for 1-hour. Roll out pastry between 2-sheets of wax paper. Peal off top sheet of paper. Invert into a 9-inch deep-dish pan. Remove paper. Flute edges. Refrigerate for 1-hour.

Prepare filling:
Preheat oven at 375-degrees
6-cups peeled, thinly sliced cooking apples, about 2-pounds
1-cup & 3-tablespoons sugar
6-tablespoons all-purpose flour
3-eggs
¾-cup butter, melt and add ½-cup chopped walnuts
2-tablespoons Kentucky Bourbon, *I use the best Kentucky Bourbon, Woodford Reserve Straight Bourbon Whiskey.*

Arrange apples in pastry shell. In a medium bowl, combine sugar, flour, and eggs. Stir with wire whisk until smooth. Slowly stir in melted butter, walnuts, and Bourbon. Pour over apples. Bake 1-hour, then cool. Before serving, sprinkle top with confectioners sugar, if desired.
Makes 8-servings.

Apple Crisp
Preheat oven at 350-degrees.
Set out baking dish.

4-cups apples, chopped
1-cup crushed pineapple
Dash of cinnamon
1-cup oats
2-cups brown sugar
½-cup flour
1-stick butter

    Mix apples and pineapple with cinnamon. Place in baking dish. Combine oats, brown sugar, flour, and butter until crumbly. Sprinkle on top of apple mixture. Bake at 350-degrees for 40-minutes or until apples are tender.

Blackberry Crisp
Long ago, blackberries grew plentifully by the roadside. We picked and sold them for 50-cents a gallon.
Preheat oven at 350-degrees.
Prepare greased glass baking dish.

4-cups blackberries
1 & ½-cups Graham Cracker crumbs
2-tablespoons brown sugar, firmly packed
1-tablespoons honey
¼-teaspoon cinnamon
⅛-teaspoon nutmeg
¼-cup butter

    Melt butter in medium saucepan. Stir in Graham Cracker crumbs and slowly add brown sugar, honey, cinnamon, and nutmeg. Stir until well blended. Pour berries into a greased glass-baking dish. Sweeten berries if desired. Top with Graham Cracker mix. Bake at 350-degrees for 20-minutes. Serve with Cool Whip or ice cream. Makes 4-servings.

Amaretto Pudding Pie

Preheat oven at 350-degrees.
Set out 9 x 13 x 2-inch pan.

1 & ½-cups all-purpose flour
1-cup pecans, finely chopped
1 & ¼-stick butter

Mix ingredients together. Press into baking pan. Bake at 350-degrees for 13-minutes or until lightly brown. Cool.

Filling:

2-cups sugar
2, 8-ounce packages cream cheese
2-cups whipped cream, La Crème or Cool Whip

Mix together until well blended. Spread over cooled crust.

Topping:

2, 3-ounce packages Vanilla Instant Pudding
1 & ½-cup milk
¼- to ½-cup Amaretto Liqueur

Mix ingredients together and spread over filling.

Garnish:

12-ounces whipped cream
3-ounces sliced almonds

Spread whipped cream over topping and garnish with almonds.

Chess Pie

I made this pie many time for my dear friend, Jean Siree.
Preheat oven to 325-degrees.
Set out unbaked 9-inch pie shell.

5-egg yolks
1-cup sugar
⅛-teaspoon salt
⅓-cup melted butter
2-tablespoons heavy cream
1-teaspoon vanilla

    Beat egg yolks until fluffy. Gradually add salt and sugar. Next, add butter, cream, and vanilla. Beat well. Turn into unbaked 9-inch pie shell. Bake at 325-degrees for 40-minutes.

Coconut Crunch Pie
From Doris Gresham
Grace Episcopal Church Cookbook
Paducah, Kentucky

Preheat oven at 350-degrees.
Prepare buttered glass pie pan.

4-egg whites, unbeaten
A pinch of salt
1-cup Graham Cracker crumbs
1-cup coconut
1-cup sugar
1-cup chopped pecans
1-teaspoon vanilla
Whipped cream
Bananas

    Beat egg whites until stiff, but not dry. Gradually add sugar, salt, and vanilla. Stir in Graham Crackers, coconut, and pecans. Pour into a buttered glass pie pan and bake at 350-degrees for 20-minutes. Do not over-bake. Serve with sliced bananas and whipped cream. You may wish to cover the entire pie with bananas and whipped cream or cover one slice at a time.

Boston Cream Pie

This dessert from Massachusetts dates back to the 1800's.

Preheat oven at 350-degrees.

Prepare 8-x 8-inch pan greased with Crisco.

1-teaspoon Crisco
½-cup milk
1-cup flour, sifted
1-teaspoon salt
2-eggs, well beaten
1-cup sugar
1-teaspoon vanilla

Cream filling:

⅔-cup sugar
⅓-cup flour
⅛-teaspoon salt
1-egg, slightly beaten
1-teaspoon vanilla

Add Crisco to milk and heat over hot water. Sift flour with baking powder and salt. Beat eggs until thick and light. Gradually beat in sugar. Fold in flour and blend thoroughly. Pour batter into pan greased with Crisco. Bake in moderate oven at 350-degrees for 40 to 50-minutes.

Mix sugar, flour, and salt. Pour on scalded milk gradually and cook over hot water until smooth and thick, about 15-minutes. Pour over beaten egg. Return to double boiler and cook 2-minutes longer. Add vanilla. Split warm cake and spread cream filling between layers. Sift confectioners sugar over top or cover with a chocolate frosting.

Blueberry Cream Pie

1, 8-inch pastry pie shell, baked
1-package vanilla pudding
1 & ½-cups milk

½-cup heavy cream, whipped
1-package (2-cups) frozen, unsweetened blueberries thawed, or 2-cups
    fresh blueberries
1-tablespoon cornstarch
2-tablespoons granulated sugar
1-tablespoon lemon rind, grated
1-tablespoon lemon juice

Early in the day, make pudding as package directs using 1 & ½-cups milk. Refrigerate until cold. Fold in whipped cream. Turn into baked pie shell. Refrigerate until cold.

Topping:

Place 1-cup blueberries in a saucepan. Combine cornstarch, sugar, lemon rind and juice and add to blueberries. Cook over low heat mashing and stirring until mixture thickens and clears. Add remaining berries. Cool slightly. Then, carefully spoon over pudding in pie shell. Refrigerate until serving time.

Fresh Blueberry Pie

Preheat oven to 400-degrees.

1, 9-inch pastry pie shell, unbaked
¾-cup sugar
1-egg
8-ounces sour cream
2-tablespoons all-purpose flour
1-teaspoon vanilla extract
¼-teaspoon salt
2 & ½-cups fresh blueberries
2-tablespoons sugar
3-tablespoons butter
3-tablespoons pecans, chopped
3-tablespoons all-purpose flour

Combine first 6-ingredients in a large mixing bowl. Beat with an electric mixer on medium speed for 5-minutes or until smooth. Spoon into pastry shell. Bake 25-minutes at 400-degrees. Combine flour and sugar. Cut in butter with pastry blender until mixture looks like coarse meal. Stir in pecans. Sprinkle over pie and bake another 15-minutes.

Impossible Pie

My sister Mabel gave me this recipe from the early days when she worked at the Magnavox Factory.

Preheat oven at 350-degrees.
Prepare greased pie pan.

2-cups milk
¾-cup sugar
½-cup Bisquick Mix
4-eggs
¼-cup butter
1 & 1 ½-teaspoon vanilla extract
1-cup coconut, shredded

Combine milk, sugar, Bisquick Mix, eggs, butter, and vanilla in mixing bowl. Blend with electric mixer at low speed for 3-minutes. Pour into greased pie pan and let stand for 5-minutes. Sprinkle top with coconut. Bake at 350-degrees for 40-minutes.

Sweet Potato Pie

Preheat oven at 300 to 350-degrees.
Use unbaked pie shell.

2-cups sweet potatoes, mashed
1-stick butter
2-eggs
1-cup sugar
½-cup orange juice
Grated orange rind to add flavor, optional

Boil, remove skin, and mash potatoes. Cream butter, eggs, and sugar. Mix potatoes with creamed mixture. Add orange juice and rind. Brush unbaked pie shell with milk and sugar before baking. Pour mixture into unbaked pie shell and bake at 300 to 350-degrees until crust is brown. During baking the filling sets around the outside edges first then gradually it firms toward the center. When you remove the pie from the oven, the center, about the size of a silver dollar, is still slightly liquid. The center continues to bake and set while cooling. You can tap the center surface with your finger the last 10-minutes of baking.

Strawberry Shortcake

2-cups all-purpose flour
1-tablespoon sugar
2-teaspoons baking powder
1-teaspoon salt
¼-cup unsalted butter, chilled and cut into small pieces
¾-cup milk

Prepare strawberries:

3-pints fresh strawberries
2-tablespoons sugar

Topping:

1-cup whipping cream
¼-teaspoon vanilla

Set aside 8-whole strawberries for garnish. Wash and quarter enough berries to measure 3-cups. Lightly toss berries with sugar. Let stand at room temperature for up to 2-hours for fruit to sweeten.

Heat oven to 425-degrees. Mix dry ingredients together in a bowl. Cut the butter into the dry mixture with 2-forks or pastry blender until dough resembles coarse meal. Stir in milk with a fork. Do not overmix. Gather in a ball. Knead dough on a lightly floured surface for 30-seconds. Roll or pat it out to ¼-inch thick.

Cut out 8-shortcakes with a 2 & ½-inch cookie or biscuit cutter. Place cakes 1-inch apart on a baking sheet. Bake at 425-degrees for 15-minutes or until lightly brown. Cut shortcakes in half with a fork or knife. Divide berries equally atop shortcake bottoms. Spoon whipped cream over berries. Cover with shortcake tops. Garnish each with whipped cream and a whole berry.

Strawberry Chiffon Pie

1-envelope gelatin
¼-cup cold water
2-egg yolks
¾-cup Karo Syrup
1-cup strawberries, crushed
1-tablespoon lemon juice
⅛-teaspoon salt
2-egg whites
¼-cup sugar
¾-cup whipped cream
1-baked 9-inch pastry shell

Soften gelatin in cold water. Slightly beat egg yolks in top of double boiler. Add Karo Syrup. Cook over boiling water about 5-minutes, stirring constantly until mixture is somewhat thickened. Add gelatin. Stir until gelatin is dissolved. Cool for a bit. Combine strawberries and lemon juice and add to gelatin mixture. Chill until slightly thickened. Add salt to egg whites and beat until stiff, but not dry. Gradually beat in sugar. Fold in strawberry mixture. Then, fold in whipped cream. Place into baked pastry shell. Chill thoroughly. Garnish with whipped cream.

Pastry shell:

Preheat oven at 375-degrees.

1-cup all-purpose flour

1-tablespoon butter, room temperature, but not soft

1-egg yolk

1-tablespoon ice water

Combine flour and sugar. Then work in butter with fingertips. Add egg yolk and ice water. Work with fingers until dough holds together, but don't overwork. Pat flat and round. Chill until firm enough to roll. Then, roll between sheets of waxed paper to fit a 9-inch loose-bottomed tart pan. Remove top paper and turn pastry over pan, centered spacing. Let pastry slip down into pan and gently pull off paper. Use fingertips to press pastry into pan. Even off the rim and chill shell. Bake at 375-degrees for about 15-minutes or until lightly browned. During baking, prick the dough with fork whenever it begins to bubble. This helps keep the shell flat. Cool before filling.

Strawberry Tart

Pastry shell, baked

1-package, 3-ounces, cream cheese, softened

3-tablespoons dairy sour cream

1 to 1 & ½-quarts strawberries

1-cup sugar

3-tablespoons cornstarch

Red food coloring, optional

Beat cream cheese until fluffy, add sour cream and beat until smooth. Spread on bottom of shell and refrigerate. Wash and hull strawberries. Mash enough uneven berries to make 1-cup. Force through sieve and add water to make 1-cup. Mix sugar and cornstarch. Add ½-cup water and sieved berries. Cook over medium heat, stirring until mixture is clear and thickened. Then boil about 1-minute. Stir to cool slightly and add a little red food coloring, if desired. Fill pastry shell with remaining berries, tips up. Pour cooked mixture over top. Chill 1-hour.

Old Fashioned Peach Cobbler
Preheat oven at 375-degrees.
Use 1 & ½-quart class dish.

1-quart fresh peaches, peeled and sliced (I prefer Elberta Freestone)
1-cup flour, sifted
1-teaspoon baking powder
⅛-teaspoon salt
1-cup sugar
1-egg
3-tablespoons milk
¼-teaspoon vanilla
Grated nutmeg

Mix peaches with ½-cup sugar. Lightly sprinkle with grated nutmeg and set aside. In another bowl, sift flour, baking powder, and salt. Cut in butter with knives or pastry blender until it breaks in very small pieces. Beat the egg and add remaining ½-cup sugar. Beat until thick. Beat in milk and vanilla. Fold gently into flour mixture. (This will not be smooth.) Spread over peaches that have been mixed with sugar. Bake at 375-degrees for about 45-minutes. Test with toothpick or cake tester until it comes out clean.

Pumpkin Chiffon Pie
1 & ½-cups canned, cooked pumpkin
¾-cup brown sugar, firmly packed
½-cup milk
3-egg yolks, beaten
½-teaspoon salt
1-teaspoon cinnamon

½-teaspoon nutmeg
1-envelope unflavored gelatin
¼-cup cold water
3-egg whites
¼-cup granulated sugar
1 baked 9-inch pie shell
Whipped cream for garnish

     Combine pumpkin, brown sugar, milk, beaten egg yolks, salt and spices in the top of a double boiler. Cook over boiling water, stirring often for about 10-minutes. Soften gelatin in cold water. Dissolve in hot pumpkin mixture. Pour into medium size bowl. Chill just until it begins to set. Beat egg whites until foamy. Add granulated sugar, 1-tablespoon at a time, beating well after each addition until meringue stands in soft peaks. Fold in pumpkin mixture. Pour into baked pie shell. Chill until firm enough to cut.

Bourbon Pecan Pie

Kentuckians' favorite pie on Derby Day.
The original recipe is copyrighted.
Preheat oven at 350-degrees.
Use 1, 9-inch pastry pie shell.

2-eggs, slightly beaten
1-cup sugar
½-cup all-purpose flour
½-cup butter, melted and cooled
1-cup pecans or walnuts, chopped
1, 6-ounce package semisweet chocolate morsels
1-teaspoon vanilla
½-cup Kentucky Bourbon
1, 9-inch pastry pie shell, unbaked
1-cup whipping cream

1-tablespoon Kentucky Bourbon
¼-cup confectioners sugar, sifted

     Combine first 4-ingredients in a medium-mixing bowl. Beat with an electric mixer just until blended. Stir in pecans, chocolate morsels, vanilla, and Bourbon. Pour into pastry shell and bake at 350-degrees for 45 to 50- minutes. Cover edges of pie loosely with foil during the last 30-minutes to prevent over-browning.

     Beat whipping cream and Bourbon until foamy. Gradually add confectioners sugar, beating until soft peaks form. Place onto pie slices as you serve.

Pecan Pie
When Dan and I first married, his cousin, Mabel Moore, gave me this recipe.

¾-cup sugar
1-heaping tablespoon flour
3-eggs, beaten
½-cup heavy cream
1-cup white syrup
½-stick butter, melted
¾-cups pecans, chopped
1-teaspoon vanilla
1, 9-inch pastry shell, unbaked

     Mix flour and sugar. Add to beaten eggs, cream, and white syrup. Mix in pecans, melted butter, and vanilla. Pour into unbaked pie shell. Bake at 350-degrees for 45-minutes to 1-hour.

Mock Pecan Pie
Preheat oven at 350-degrees.

⅔-cup regular oats, uncooked

⅔-cup light corn syrup

2-eggs, beaten

1-teaspoon vanilla

¼-teaspoon salt

⅔-cup butter, melted and cooled

1, 8-inch pastry shell, unbaked

Combine oats, corn syrup, eggs, vanilla, and salt. Mix well. Add melted butter and mix thoroughly. Pour into pastry shell and bake 1-hour at 350-degrees. Cool before serving.

Old Fashioned Rice Pudding
Preheat oven at 300-degrees.

Use flat baking dish.

Combine all ingredients in a flat baking dish and place in a slow oven at 300-degrees. Bake 1 & ½-hours or until rice is tender and pudding is thick and creamy, but not dry. Stir every 15-minutes with a fork, carefully turning under the browned topping and scraping the edges of the pan. Serve hot or cold. Yield: 5-servings.

Curried Fruit
Preheat oven at 325-degrees.

Use a 13 x 9 x 1-inch baking dish.

1, 16-ounce can sliced Freestone peaches, drained

1, 16-ounce can pear halves, drained

1, 17-ounce can apricot halves, drained

1, 16-ounce can pitted dark sweet cherries, drained

1, 15-ounce can pineapple chunks, drained

⅔-cup slivered almonds

¾-cup light brown sugar, firmly packed
1-tablespoon curry powder
⅓-cup melted butter

    Layer fruit in a 13 x 9 x 1-inch baking dish. Sprinkle with almonds. Combine brown sugar and curry powder. Stir in melted butter and spoon over fruit. Bake at 325-degrees for 1-hour. Cool. Refrigerate overnight. Bake at 350-degrees for 20-minutes or until bubbly. Yield: 8-servings.

Syllabub
This dish is English in origin dating back to the time of Elizabeth I.
Prepare a day ahead.
Use parfait glasses.

3-cups whipping cream
Juice and rind of 4-lemons
1-cup sugar
1-cup white wine
½-cup dry sherry
Whipped cream for topping

    Whisk the whipping cream by hand until it thickens a bit. In order, add lemon rind, lemon juice, sugar, white wine, and sherry one at a time. Whisk by hand after each addition. Whisk the mixture for 3 to 5-minutes until thickened. Keep in mind that too much whipping will turn cream into butter. Pour immediately into parfait glasses and refrigerate overnight. It will separate into layers. If desired, pile whipped cream on the top of each glass before serving. Makes 12 to 16-servings.

Russian Cream
A wonderful cook and dear person, Fran Cicansky, my daughter's friend, gave me this recipe when we had dinner with her and her family in Regina, Saskatchewan.

¾-cup extra fine sugar

½-cup water

1-envelope unflavored gelatin

1-cup whipping cream

1 & ½-cups Crème Fraiche, or sour cream

1-teaspoon vanilla extract

Strawberries, for garnish

    Combine sugar, water, and gelatin in a small saucepan. Blend well. Let stand 4 to 5-minutes. Place over medium heat and bring to a boil, stirring constantly. Remove from heat. Gradually blend in cream. Combine sour cream and vanilla in a medium bowl. Gradually add hot sugar mixture, whisking until smooth. Pour into wine or sherbet glasses. Cover and refrigerate 4 to 6-hours. Garnish with strawberries and serve.

Mama's Buttermilk Sherbet

    When we got our first refrigerator in the 1930's, Mama created many dishes she could make in the freezer. For this recipe, she put the mixture in the ice cube tray without the cube sections. It made a great dessert on a hot summer day.

1, 8-ounce can crushed pineapple, do not drain

1-cup sugar

2-cups buttermilk

1-tablespoon vanilla extract

2-egg whites

    Beat egg whites until stiff, but not dry. Mix pineapple, sugar, buttermilk, and vanilla. Freeze until mushy. Add egg whites to the mixture and return to ice trays. Cover and freeze.

CAKES, ICINGS & FROSTINGS

Graham Cracker Cake
My sister, Mabel made this cake during the 1930's - 1940's.
Preheat oven at 375-degrees. Prepare 2, 9-inch layer pans with Crisco, or line with heavy wax paper.

1 & ½-cups flour, sifted
⅔-cup Crisco
1 & ½-cups finely crushed graham cracker crumbs (almost to powder)
1 & ½-cups sugar
1-teaspoon salt
¾-cup milk

Combine above ingredients in a large bowl. Beat at medium speed on electric mixer for 2 minutes. Stir in 3 & ½-teapooons double-acting baking powder. Add 3-eggs, ½-cup milk, 1-teaspoon vanilla. Mix all thoroughly with mixer on medium speed for 2-minutes

Pour into 2, 9-inch layer pans (1 & ½-inches deep) that has been rubbed with Crisco or lined with heavy waxed paper. Bake in moderate oven at 375- degrees for 30 to 35-minutes. When layers are cool, apply Creamy Lemon icing between layers and on top and sides.

Creamy Lemon Icing:
¼-cup granulated sugar
2-tablespoons lemon juice
2 & ⅓-cups sifted confectioners sugar
1-egg
½-cup Crisco
1-tablespoon grated lemon rind

Mix confectioners sugar and egg thoroughly. Bring lemon juice and granulated sugar to a boil. Boil 1-minute. Add to sugar and egg mixture. Blend well. Add Crisco and lemon rind. Beat until creamy.

Sour Cream Pound Cake
Grease and flour large tube pan.
Preheat oven to 300-degrees.

1-cup butter
3-cups sugar
6-eggs, separated
¼-teaspoon salt
3-cups flour, sifted
½-pint sour cream

Cream butter and sugar thoroughly. Add egg yolks one at a time. Add salt to flour. Alternately add flour and sour cream to creamed mixture. Beat egg whites until stiff and fold in. Bake in prepared pan at 300-degrees for 1 & ½-hours or until a toothpick inserted in the center of the cake comes out clean. Top of cake should have a nice brown crust. Let stand for 15-minutes before taking it out of the pan. No flavoring needed. In a day or so, the cake increases in moistness.

Kentucky Pound Cake
Grease and flour a 10-inch tube pan.
Preheat oven to 350-degrees.

2 & ½-cups self-rising flour
2-cups granulated sugar
4-eggs
1 & ¼-cups vegetable oil
1-cup pecans, chopped
1-teaspoon pure vanilla extract
1, 8-ounce can crushed pineapple packed in syrup

Mix flour, granulated sugar, eggs, oil, pecans, vanilla, and crushed pineapple with the syrup in a bowl. Blend and pour into prepared pan. Bake for 1 hour & 15-minutes or until a toothpick inserted in the center of the cake comes out clean. Remove cake from pan and cool.

Frosting:

2-cups confectioners sugar

4-tablespoons margarine, softened

4-ounces cream cheese, softened

    Blend confectioners sugar, margarine, and cream cheese in mixing bowl. Spread on cooled cake.

Sour Cream Coconut Cake

Prepare cake at least 3-days before serving.

Prepare icing:

2-cups sour cream

1 & ¼-cups sugar

1-teaspoon pure almond extract (optional)

1, 8-ounce package Cool Whip

3, 6-ounce packages frozen, flaked coconut, use 2-packages in icing and save the 3rd-package to sprinkle over outside cake

    By hand, mix sour cream, sugar, flavor, and 2-packages coconut. Fold in Cool Whip. Refrigerate overnight.

Prepare cake:

1-box yellow or white cake mix

    Prepare according to directions, using milk instead of water. Bake as directed for 2, 9-inch layers. Cool. Slice into 4-layers.

    Spread icing over cake layers. Sprinkle coconut over top and sides of cake. Refrigerate at least 48-hours.

White Cake

Preheat oven at 350-degrees.

    Grease 2, 8-inch layer pans with Crisco and dust with flour.

½-cup Crisco

¾-teaspoon salt

½-teaspoon grated lemon rind

1-cup sugar

2 & ½-teaspoons baking powder

2 & ¼-cups sifted flour

¾-cup milk

3-egg whites

    Combine Crisco, salt, and lemon rind. Blend. Add sugar gradually and cream until light and fluffy. Add baking powder to flour. Sift 3-times. Add small amounts of flour to creamed mixture, alternating with milk and mixing after each addition until smooth. Beat egg whites until stiff, but not dry. Fold carefully into mixture until well blended. Pour into prepared pans and bake 25 to 30-minutes.

                      Lemon filling:

¾-cup sugar

3-tablespoons flour

Pinch salt

¼-cup lemon juice

Grated rind of 1-lemon

½-cup water

3-egg yolks

2-tablespoons butter

    Combine sugar, flour, and salt. Mix thoroughly. Add lemon juice and lemon rind, mixing well. Add water, egg yolks, and butter. Blend. Place over hot water and cook until smooth and thick for about 15-minutes, stirring constantly. Cool and spread between cake layers. Sprinkle grated lemon rind over filling. Dust top of cake with confectioners sugar.

Chocolate Fudge Cake

Lightly grease 9 x 13 x 2-inch baking pan.
Preheat oven at 350-degrees.

1 & ¾-cups flour
2-cups brown sugar, packed
¾-cup cocoa, measured, then sifted
2-teaspoons baking powder
Dash salt
2-eggs
¼-cup vegetable oil
1-cup cola soda
1-cup buttermilk
1-teaspoon vanilla

Sift flour, brown sugar, cocoa, baking soda, baking powder, and salt in a large bowl. In the center, add eggs, cola soda, buttermilk, and vanilla. Whisk about 3-minutes to make a smooth thin batter. Pour into a lightly greased baking pan. Bake for 30 to 45-minutes at 350-degrees or until cake tests done. Cool on counter. Refrigerate while preparing icing. Cut into squares.

Cola frosting:

¼-cup unsalted butter
3-tablespoons cocoa
⅓-cup cola soda
4-cups confectioners sugar

Combine butter, cocoa, cola soda, and confectioners' sugar in a bowl. Whip or beat until fluffy and smooth.

Lemon Pudding Cake

Set out 8 x 8 x 2-inch baking pan and a larger pan for hot water.
¼-cup all-purpose flour, sifted
Dash salt

¾-cup sugar
3-tablespoons melted butter
1-teaspoon lemon peel, grated
¼-cup lemon juice
1 & ½-cups milk
3-egg yolks, well beaten
3-egg whites, stiffly beaten

     Combine flour, salt, and sugar. Stir in melted butter, lemon peel, and lemon juice. Combine milk, and well-beaten egg yolks. Add to lemon mixture. Fold in egg whites. Pour into baking pan. Place baking pan in a larger pan. Pour hot water into the larger pan 1-inch deep. Bake at 350-degrees for 40-minutes. Serve warm or cold. Yield: 8 to 9-servings.

Lemon Nut Cake
Excellent cake for Thanksgiving or Christmas dinner.
Preheat oven at 300-degrees.
Grease and flour a 10-inch tube pan, or 2, 9 x 5 x 3-inch loaf pans.

1-pound butter or margarine
2-cups sugar
6-eggs, separated
1, 3-ounce bottle lemon extract
1-teaspoon baking soda
1-teaspoon warm water
5-cups all-purpose flour, sifted
3-cups pecans, chopped
1, 15-ounce box golden raisins

     Cream butter and sugar until light and fluffy. Add egg yolks, beating well. Stir in lemon extract. Dissolve baking soda in warm water. Add to creamed mixture along with flour, blending well. Stir in pecans and raisins. Beat egg whites until stiff and fold into batter. Pour in prepared pan(s). Bake at 300-degrees for 2-hours or until cake tests done.

Pumpkin Cake

I made this cake many times for my daughter to take to school for her teachers at Thanksgiving.

Grease 2, round, 8-inch pans and line with wax paper.

Preheat oven at 350-degrees.

2 & ¼-cups cake flour
3-tablespoons baking powder
¼-teaspoon baking soda
1 & ½-teaspoon cinnamon
½-teapoon ginger
½-teaspoon allspice
½-cup shortening or butter
1-cup brown sugar, firmly packed
½-cup granulated sugar
1-egg and 2-egg yolks, unbeaten
¾-cup buttermilk
¾-cup canned pumpkin
½-cup walnuts, finely chopped

Measure sifted flour and add baking powder, salt, soda, and spices. Sift together 3-times. Cream butter, add sugars gradually and cream well. Add egg and egg yolks, one at a time, beating until light. Add flour alternating with buttermilk in small amounts, beating after each addition until smooth. Add pumpkin and nuts. Mix well. Bake in prepared pans for 30 to 35- minutes at 350-degrees. Cool and frost with orange-tinted fluffy frosting.

Queen Elizabeth Cake

Recipe given to me by a south Florida friend.

Grease 9 x 12-inch pan.

Preheat oven at 350-degrees.

1-teaspoon baking soda
1-cup boiling water

1-cup chopped dates
1-cup sugar
¼-cup butter
1-egg, beaten
1-teaspoon vanilla
1 & ½-cups all-purpose flour, sifted
1-teaspoon baking powder
½-teaspoon salt
½-cup pecans, chopped

Put soda in boiling water and pour over dates. Let stand while mixing the batter. Cream sugar and butter. Add egg, then vanilla. Sift dry ingredients together and gradually add to batter. Add nuts and date mixture. Mix well. Bake in prepared pan at 350-degrees for 35-minutes.

Frosting:

Combine ingredients and boil for 3-minutes:
5-tablespoons brown sugar
5-tablespoons light cream
2-tablespoons butter
Grated coconut

Spread on cake without beating. Sprinkle with grated coconut.

Jam Cake

Grease 2, 9-inch square pans, 2-inches deep, and line with wax paper. Preheat oven at 350-degrees.

2-cups granulated sugar
4-cups flour
1-cup shortening
1-teaspoon baking powder
½-cup buttermilk
2-cups strawberry jam
6-whole eggs

½-teaspoon nutmeg

1-teaspoon cinnamon

1-teaspoon allspice

1-teaspoon baking soda

Cream the shortening with sugar and beat until fluffy. Sift flour, measure and sift again with baking powder and spices. Beat eggs and add to sugar and shortening mixture. Next, add jam and beat well. Dissolve baking soda in buttermilk and add to the mixture alternating with the spice and flour mixture. Pour batter into prepared pans and bake at 350-degrees for 50-minutes.

Caramel Icing for Jam Cake:

2-cups brown sugar

6-tablespoons butter

1-teaspoon vanilla

6-tablespoons evaporated milk

¼-teaspoon salt

Mix all ingredients, except vanilla. Allow mixture to come to a boil, stirring constantly. Remove from heat, cool slightly, and beat until smooth and creamy. Add vanilla and spread between layers, on sides, and top of cake.

Mama's Pecan Hash for Jam Cake

You may wish to use this topping instead of Caramel Icing.

1-cup candied cherries, chopped

1-cup pecans, chopped

1-cup raisins, chopped

1-cup coconut, grated

2 & ¾-cups custard

Custard:

2-cups milk

4-egg yolks

½-cup sugar

⅓-cup cornstarch

1-teaspoon vanilla

    Combine the first 4-ingredients in a heavy saucepan. Stir with a wire whisk until well blended. Cook over medium heat, stirring constantly until thickened and smooth. Stir in vanilla. Chill. Add cherries, pecans, raisins, and coconut. Spread between layers, on sides, and top. Makes the cake especially moist.

Great Depression Cake

This recipe became popular after the stock market crash of 1929. There are several versions of this cake.

Generously grease 2, 3 x 9 x 2-inch pans.

Preheat oven at 350-degrees.

2-cups sugar

2-cups strong coffee

½-cup shortening

2-cups raisins

1-apple, peeled and grated

1-cup candied fruit mix, diced

2-cups all-purpose flour

1-teaspoon baking soda

2-teaspoons baking powder

1-teaspoon, each, cinnamon, nutmeg, allspice

1-cup walnuts, chopped

    In a large saucepan, simmer the first 5-ingredients for 10-minutes, stirring occasionally. Cool 10-minutes. Blend together the remaining ingredients and stir into mixture. Pour batter into prepared pans. Bake at 350-degrees for 25 to 30-minutes. Test for doneness. Cool and dust with powdered sugar.

Apple Pie Cake with Rum Butter Sauce
Grease and flour a 9-inch pie plate.
Preheat oven at 350-degrees.

¼-cup butter, softened

1-cup sugar

1-egg

1-cup all-purpose flour

1-teaspoon salt

1-teaspoon ground cinnamon

2-tablespoons hot water

1-teaspoon vanilla

3-cups cooking apples, peeled and diced

½-cup pecans, chopped

Cream butter. Gradually add sugar, beating well at medium speed with an electric mixer. Add egg. Beat until blended. Combine flour, salt, and cinnamon. Mix well. Add to mixture. Beat on low speed with an electric mixer until smooth. Stir in water and vanilla. Fold in apples and pecans. Spoon into prepared pans. Bake at 350-degrees for 45-minutes or until a toothpick inserted in the center comes out clean. Serve warm or cold with Rum Butter Sauce and whipped cream, if desired.

Rum Butter Sauce:

½-cup brown sugar, firmly packed

¼-cup butter, softened

1-tablespoon Rum

½-cup sugar

½-cup whipping cream

Yield: 1 & ¼-cups.

Pumpkin Roll
Grease 5 & ½-inch x 10 & ½-inch jelly roll pan.
Line pan with greased and floured wax paper.
Preheat oven to 375-degrees.

6-eggs, at room temperature, separated
1-cup sugar, divided
1-cup all-purpose flour
1-cup canned pumpkin
1-teaspoon ground cinnamon
1-teaspoon double-acting baking powder
1-teaspoon ground ginger
½-teaspoon ground nutmeg
½-teaspoon salt
Approximately 4-cups confectioners sugar
2, 8-ounce packages cream cheese, softened
1-teaspoon vanilla extract
1-cup walnuts, chopped

    Place egg whites in a large bowl. Set mixer at high speed and beat until soft peaks form. Continue beating at high speed. Gradually add in ½-cup sugar, 2-tablespoons at a time, beating after each addition until sugar is dissolved. Whites should stand in stiff, glossy peaks.

    Set mixer at low speed. Beat the following ingredients in a small bowl, flour, pumpkin, cinnamon, baking powder, ginger, nutmeg, ½-cup sugar, ½-teaspoon salt, and egg yolks, until well blended.

    With a wire whisk or rubber spatula, gently fold in pumpkin mixture into egg white mixture. Spread half of batter evenly into jelly roll pan. Set remaining batter aside. Bake 12-minutes or until top of cake springs back when touched with finger.

    Meanwhile, sprinkle a clean tea cloth towel with some confectioners sugar. When cake is done, invert it immediately onto prepared towel. Carefully peel off waxed paper. Starting at the narrow end, roll cake with towel in a jellyroll fashion. Place cake seam side down on wire rack. Cool about 1 & ½- hours.

While cake is cooling, re-line the same jellyroll pan with greased, floured wax paper. Spread remaining batter evenly in cake pan. As before, bake 12-minutes, prepare roll, and cool.

Prepare filling:

Set mixer at low speed. In a separate small bowl, beat cream cheese, vanilla, 3-cups confectioners sugar and ½-teaspoon salt until well blended. Stir in walnuts.

Gently unroll cooled cakes. Evenly spread half of the cream cheese mixture on each cake, almost to the edge. Starting at the narrow end, re-roll each cake without the towel. Place cake roll seam side down on a large platter. Cover and refrigerate until chilled, about 1-hour. To serve, sprinkle tops of rolls lightly with confectioners sugar.
Makes 2-rolls, about 20-servings.

Punch Bowl Cake

1, 20-ounce Angel Food cake, broken into small pieces
2- boxes frozen strawberries, thawed
2, 3 & ½-ounce packages instant vanilla pudding, prepare according to directions on the box
5-bananas
1, 16-ounce container, Cool Whip

Make layers of cake, strawberries, bananas, pudding, and Cool Whip in a glass bowl, using half the ingredients. Repeat with a second layer, ending with Cool Whip on top. Refrigerate until ready to serve.

Banana Sponge Cake

Use 10-inch tube pan, do not grease.
Preheat oven to 350-degrees.

1 & ½-cups sugar
2-teaspoons baking powder

1-teaspoon salt
½-cup cooking oil
6-eggs, separated
1-cup mashed bananas
1-teaspoon lemon juice
2 & ¼-cups all-purpose flour
½-teaspoon cream of tartar

 Mix sugar, baking powder, and salt in a large mixing bowl. Add oil and egg yolks. Beat until mixed well and smooth. Add bananas and lemon juice and mix well. Beat egg whites and cream of tartar until stiff. Fold into batter, but do not stir! Pour into tube pan. Bake at 350-degrees for 1-hour and 5-minutes. Turn pan upside down to cool. When completely cool, remove from pan to cake plate.

Peanut Rolls

Mama and the ladies of Trinity Baptist Church made these delicious rolls so many times, especially for Christmas.
I would help sell them for 25-cents a dozen.

Dust flour in the bottom of 8 x 8 x 2-inch cake pan, do not grease.
Preheat oven at 350-degrees.

2-egg, separated
1-cup granulated sugar, sifted
½-cup flour, sifted
1-rounded teaspoon, baking powder
½-teaspoon vanilla
½-cup boiling water

 Beat egg yolks, add 1-cup sifted granulated sugar, and mix well. Add ½-cup sifted flour. Fold in beaten egg whites. Add another ½-cup sifted flour with 1-rounded teaspoon of baking powder. Add vanilla. Last, add ½- cup boiling water. Pour into prepared pan. Bake at 350-degrees for about 20 to 25-minutes. Cool and cut into 12-squares with a wet knife.

Icing:

Sift a 1-pound box of confectioners sugar. Mix it with water thin enough to dip all sides of the cake squares. As you do this, place each one on a cake rack. Grind about 2-pounds of Spanish peanuts, ½-cup at a time, in a blender. Sprinkle cake squares generously on all sides.

Cream Cheese Cupcakes

Given to me by Janet Andrews, a sweet young lady. We worked together at JC Penny's before she went away to college.

Set out 24-large or 48-mini size paper baking cups.

Preheat oven at 300-degrees.

3, 8-ounce packages cream cheese, room temperature

1-cup granulated sugar

5-eggs

1 & ½-teaspoon vanilla

Mix and beat all ingredients. Pour into paper baking cups ⅔-full. Bake at 300-degrees for 20 to 25-minutes or until tops break open. Remove from oven and cool.

Topping:

1-cup sour cream

½-cup granulated sugar

½-teaspoon vanilla

Maraschino cherries

Mix the first 3-ingredients above and spoon on top of cupcakes. Spread topping and place a halved Maraschino cherry in the center of each. Bake 5-minutes. Remove from oven and cool. Refrigerate until ready to serve. Makes 24-large or 48-mini cupcakes.

Fruitcake Cupcakes

Grease and flour mini size muffin pans.
Preheat oven at 375-degrees.

⅓-cup Crisco

1-cup sugar

2-eggs

2-cups flour, sifted

1-cup sour cream

1-teaspoon cinnamon

1-teaspoon nutmeg

¼-teaspoon cloves, ground

1-teaspoon baking soda

¼-cup pecans, chopped

½-cup candied cherries, chopped

½-cup candied green and yellow pineapple, or 1 & ½-slice of each

½-cup dates, chopped

Cream Crisco and sugar together. Add sour cream and eggs. Beat well. Combine remaining ingredients and add gradually. Pour into prepared pans. Bake at 375-degrees for 15-minutes

Biscuit Pudding

Mama used leftover biscuits to make Biscuit Pudding.
Biscuits are no longer made from scratch in most kitchens.

Grease 9-inch baking pan.
Preheat oven at 350-degrees.

3-cups biscuits, crumbled

2-cups milk, scalded

1-tablespoon butter

¼-teaspoon salt

¾-cup sugar

2-eggs, beaten

½-teaspoon nutmeg

1-teaspoon vanilla

½-cup raisins

½- cup crushed pineapple, drained

     Soak biscuits in milk about 5-minutes. Add butter, salt, and sugar. Pour slowly over beaten eggs. Add vanilla and nutmeg. Mix well. Fold in raisins and pineapple. Pour into prepared pan. Bake at 350-degrees for 40-minutes or until a knife inserted comes out clean.

Fruit Ambrosia

     Cut selected fruit, such as orange slices, banana, and pineapple. Sprinkle with confectioners sugar. Chill. Serve plain or top with toasted, shredded coconut or maraschino cherries, just before serving.

Caramel Frosting

½-cup butter or margarine

1-cup brown sugar, firmly packed

¼-cup whipping cream

2 & ½-cups confectioners sugar, sifted

1-teaspoon vanilla

     Melt butter in a heavy saucepan. Add brown sugar. Cook over low heat, stirring constantly until dissolved. Do not boil! Remove from heat. Stir in whipping cream. Add powdered sugar and vanilla. Beat until smooth with electric mixer set at high speed. Yields enough to frost a 10-inch cake or one with 2, 9-inch layers. If the Caramel Frosting becomes too firm to spread, place over low heat, stirring constantly, until it is thin and back to spreading consistency.

Fudge Icing

1-pound confectioners sugar

6-tablespoons butter

½-cup unsweetened cocoa
¼-cup milk
1-tablespoon vanilla
¼-teaspoon salt

In a medium saucepan, heat sugar, butter, cocoa, milk, vanilla, and salt over low heat, stirring until smooth. Yields enough to frost a cake with 2, 8-inch layers.

Cream Cheese Icing

1-stick butter, softened
1, 8-ounce package cream cheese, softened
1-box confectioners sugar, sifted
1-teaspoon vanilla

Mix ingredients thoroughly. You may wish to add cocoa, coconut, or pecans according to your taste. This is great on a yellow, carrot, or Red Velvet cake. Yields enough to frost a 3-layer 8 or 9-inch cake.

Butter Icing

2-cups confectioners sugar, sifted
½-cup butter
2-tablespoons cream
1-teaspoon vanilla

Blend sugar and butter. Stir in cream and vanilla. Mix until smooth. Yields enough to frost a 2-layer cake, one baked in a 9 x 13 x 2-inch pan, or 24-cupcakes.

Chocolate Icing

Prepare according to Butter Icing. Add 2-ounces melted, unsweetened chocolate to sugar and butter. Mix until smooth.

Orange Icing

1-pound box confectioners sugar

½-cup butter

⅛-teaspoon salt

4 & ½-tablespoons orange juice

1 & ½-tablespoons orange rind, grated

    Combine sugar, butter, salt, and orange juice in top of a double boiler over simmering water. Blend until smooth. Remove from heat. Add orange rind. Cool, stirring frequently, until frosting reaches desired consistency for spreading. Yields enough to frost a 2-layer, 8-inch cake or cake baked in a 10-inch tube pan.

Peppermint Frosting

1, 3-ounce package cream cheese

1-tablespoon milk

2 & ½-cups confectioners sugar, sifted

3-tablespoons peppermint candy sticks, crushed

2-tablespoons melted butter

½-teaspoon peppermint extract

    Yields enough to frost any 2 or 3-layer cake.

Whipped Cream Frosting

1-pint heavy cream

⅓-cup confectioners sugar, sifted

1-teaspoon vanilla, or ½ to 1-teaspooon almond extract

    In a small bowl, beat cream until soft peaks form. Add sugar and vanilla, or almond extract. Beat until stiff.

No Cook Frosting for Coconut Cake

2-egg whites

1-teaspoon vanilla

¼-cup sugar
¾-cup light corn syrup
Shredded coconut

In a small mixing bowl, beat egg whites and vanilla. Beat with electric mixer set at medium speed until soft peaks form for about 1-minute. Gradually beat in sugar until stiff peaks form. Gradually add light corn syrup beating with mixer on high speed to make stiff peaks. Sprinkle with shredded coconut.

Fluffy Frosting

3-egg whites
1 & ¼-cups granulated sugar
6-teaspoons water
⅛-teaspoon cream of tartar
1-teaspoon vanilla

Remove eggs from refrigerator. Let stand at room temperature for 30-minutes. Separate eggs and place whites in a medium sized mixing bowl removing any speck of yolk. Cook sugar, water, and cream of tartar in a small saucepan over low heat stirring until dissolved. Then cook, without stirring, to 260-degrees on a candy thermometer or until a bit of syrup dropped in cold water forms a hard ball. Set syrup aside. Beat egg whites with electric beater until moist peaks are formed when beater is raised. Add syrup gradually while continuing to beat until mixture forms stiff peaks as you raise the beater. Add vanilla. Yields enough to frost 2, 8- or 9-inch layers.

Brandy Ice
This makes a great light dessert.

Vanilla ice cream, softened
1 & ½-ounce French Brandy
1-ounce White Cream de Cocoa

Fill blender half full with soft vanilla ice cream. Add French Brandy and White Cream de Cocoa. Blend to a semi-liquid. Serve in a Champagne glass with a dash of ground nutmeg with light, crisp, cookies on the side.

CANDY & COOKIES

Mama's Cinnamon Strips
Mama made this delicious treat from left over pie dough.
Preheat oven at 350-degrees.
Use a cookie sheet.

Roll out dough to 1-inch thick and cut into strips 5 to 6-inches long. Place on a cookie sheet and sprinkle with sugar mixed with cinnamon. Bake at 350-degrees for about 10-minutes or until lightly browned.

Cheese Pepper Cookies
Prepare oven at 350-degrees.

1-stick margarine
1-cup pecans, chopped
1-pound sharp cheddar cheese, finely grated
2-cups all purpose flour
1-teaspoon salt
Ground red pepper, to taste

Cream cheese and butter together. Add flour, salt, and red pepper. Mix well. Add pecans. Roll in sausage-like roll. Chill in freezer for 30-minutes to 1-hour. Slice thinly. Bake at 350-degrees for 10-minutes.

Date Nut Balls

1, 8-ounce box chopped dates
1-stick margarine
1-cup granulated sugar
2-teaspoons vanilla
1-cup chopped pecans
2-cups Rice Krispies

Melt butter, sugar, and dates. Cook slowly for 10-minutes, stirring often. Remove from heat and add other ingredients. Cool and roll into balls. Roll in confectioners sugar.

Spider Cookies
This recipe is from my dear sister-in-law, Thelma.
Prepare a cookie sheet lined with wax paper.

1, 6-ounce package butterscotch bits
1/3-cup peanut butter
1, 3-ounce can of Chow Mein Noodles
1 & ½-cup mini marshmallows

Melt butterscotch bits in a double boiler. Add peanut butter. Next add marshmallows and noodles. Mix well. Drop from spoon onto a cookie Refrigerate a few minutes before serving.

Fruit Cake Cookies
Preheat oven at 275-degrees.
Use mini bonbon paper cups and a cookie sheet.

1-pound mixed candied fruit
½-cup plain flour
1, 3-ounce can coconut
2-cups chopped pecans
1-can sweetened condensed milk

Dredge fruit in flour. Add salt, coconut, and nuts. Add milk and mix thoroughly. Bake in mini bonbon paper cups. Place them on a cookie sheet. Bake 25 to 30-minutes at 275-degrees. While still warm, place a half-size red or green candied cherry atop each cookie.

Potato Chip Cookies
Preheat oven at 350 degrees.
Use cookie sheet.

1-cup (2 sticks) softened butter or margarine
½-cup sugar
1-teaspoon vanilla
1-teaspoon crushed potato chips
1-cup all purpose flour

    Mix margarine, sugar, and vanilla together. Blend well. Add potato chips and stir in flour. Form small balls and place on cookie sheet - do not grease. Press balls flat with the bottom of a glass that has been dipped in sugar. Dip class in water first, so the sugar will stick. Bake 16 to 18-minutes, or until lightly browned. Yield: 2-dozen.

Oatmeal Raisin Cookies
Preheat oven at 350 degrees.
Use cookie sheet.

1-cup (2 sticks) softened butter or margarine
½-cup granulated sugar
2-eggs
1-teaspoon vanilla
1 & ½-cups all-purpose flour
1-teaspoon baking soda
1-teaspoon cinnamon
½-teaspoon allspice
½-teaspoon salt
3-cups quick-cooking Quaker Oats, uncooked
1-cup raisins
1-cup chocolate chips
¾-cup pecans, chopped

    Beat sugar and butter until creamy. Add eggs and vanilla. Beat well. Combine flour, baking soda, cinnamon, and salt and add to mixture. Mix well. Stir in oats, raisins, chocolate chips, and pecans. Mix well. Drop by rounded tablespoon onto cookie sheet, do not grease. Bake 10 to 12-

minutes or until lightly brown in a 350-degree oven. Cool on rack. Yield: 4-dozen.

Pecan Dainties
Preheat oven at 325-degrees.
Use cookie sheet.

1-cup softened butter
½-cup sugar
2-cups sifted flour
1-teaspoon vanilla
1-tablespoon water
2-cups ground pecans
Confectioners sugar, sifted

Cream butter and sugar until light. Add remaining ingredients. Mix well. Shape into ¾-inch balls. Bake at 325-degrees for 20-minutes. Roll while slightly warm in sifted confectioners sugar. Store in airtight container.

Christmas Lizzie's
Preheat oven at 300-degrees.
Prepare greased cookie sheet.

1-pound candied red cherries, chopped
1, 8-ounce package dates, chopped
½-pound candied green pineapples, chopped
2-cups pecans, chopped
1 & ½-cups all-purpose flour, divided
¼-cup softened butter
½-cup sugar
2-eggs
½-teaspoon baking soda
¼-teaspoon cinnamon

¼-teaspoon ground clove
¼-teaspoon ground allspice
¼-teaspoon salt
1 & ½-tablespoons milk
3-tablespoons Kentucky Bourbon

      Combine fruit and pecans. Dredge in 1-cup of flour and set aside. Cream butter, add sugar, and beat at medium speed with an electric mixer. Add eggs and beat well. Combine remaining flour, baking soda, and spices. Add to creamed mixture. Mix well. Stir in milk and Bourbon. Add fruit mixture and mix well. Batter will be stiff. Chill dough in refrigerator for about 1-hour. Drop chilled dough in heaping teaspoons onto lightly greased cookie sheet. Bake for 20 to 25-minutes at 300-degrees until lightly brown. Makes about 8-dozen cookies.

Candy Cane Cookies
Preheat oven at 375-degrees.
Use cookie sheet.

½-cup butter
½-cup shortening
1-cup confectioners sugar, sifted
1-egg
1 & ½-teaspoons almond extract
2 & ½-cups flour
1-teaspoon salt
½-teaspoon red food coloring
½-cup peppermint candy, crushed
½-cup granulated sugar

      Combine butter, shortening, confectioners sugar, egg, and extracts. Mix well. Stir in flour and salt. Divide dough in half. Blend food coloring into ½ of mixture. Roll 1-teaspoon of each color of dough into pencil-shaped strips 4-inches long. Place strips side by side. Press together lightly and twist as for ropes. Place on cookie sheet, do not grease. Curve one end of each strip to form the candy cane shape. Repeat with remaining dough. Bake for about 9-minutes at 375-degrees. Remove while warm from cookie sheet. Mix together peppermint candy and sugar. Sprinkle over cookies. Yield: 4-dozen.

Toffee Squares
Preheat oven at 350-degrees.
Prepare greased 10 x 15 x 1-inch pan.

1-cup butter
1-cup brown sugar
1-egg yolk
1-teaspoon vanilla
¼-teaspoon salt
2-cups flour
1 & ½-cups chocolate chips, melted
½-cup chopped nuts

Cream butter and add sugar gradually. Blend in egg yolk, vanilla, salt, and flour. Spread in greased 10 x 15 x 1-inch pan. Bake at 350-degrees about 20-minutes. Spread while hot with melted chocolate. Sprinkle with chopped nuts. Cool and cut in small squares. Makes 6-dozen.

Brownies
Preheat oven at 350-degrees.
Prepare 8-x 8 x 2-inch pan with Crisco and flour.

½-cup Crisco
2-ounces chocolate
¾-cup sifted flour
½-teaspoon baking powder
½-teaspoon salt

2-eggs, well beaten
1-cup sugar
1-teaspoon vanilla
1-cup pecans, coarsely chopped

    Melt Crisco and chocolate together over hot water. Cool. Sift flour with baking powder and salt. Beat eggs until light. Add sugar to chocolate mixture and blend. Add flour, vanilla, and pecans. Mix well. Pour batter into 8 x 8 x 2-inch pan. Bake in moderate oven at 350-degrees for 35-minutes. Cut into squares before removing from pan. Makes 16-brownies. Add a scoop of ice cream on each square.

Kentucky Colonel Candy

½-cup butter, softened
3-tablespoons sweetened condensed milk
⅓-cup plus 2-teaspoons Kentucky Bourbon
7 & ½-cups confectioners sugar, sifted
½-cup pecans, finely chopped
1, 6-ounce package semisweet chocolate morsels
1-tablespoon melted paraffin
Pecan halves

    Combine butter, condensed milk, and Bourbon in a large bowl. Add sugar and knead until mixture is well blended and does not stick to hands. Knead in pecans. Shape into 1-inch ball. Combine chocolate morsels and paraffin in top of double boiler. Place over hot water, stirring until chocolate is melted. Using a toothpick, dip each ball of candy into chocolate mixtures. Place on wax paper. Remove toothpick and press pecan half on each. Makes about 6-dozen.

Kentucky Bourbon Balls

1-cup confectioners sugar, sifted
1-cup Vanilla Wafer crumbs

½-cup unsweetened cocoa powder
3-tablespoons white corn syrup
½-cup Kentucky Bourbon
1-cup pecans, chopped
Unsweetened cocoa powder and confectioners sugar for coating

     Combine crumbs, sugar, cocoa powder, corn syrup, and Bourbon. Place in a food processor or electric mixer. Blend until thoroughly mixed. Then, using a spoon, stir in pecans. Roll tablespoons of mixture to form a small size ball. If the mixture is too dry to roll, add a little more corn syrup. Roll Bourbon balls in cocoa to coat them. Just before serving, dust with confectioners sugar with a strainer or shaker. Store in an airtight container and refrigerate or freeze.

Caramel Candy

     Cover a can of sweetened condensed milk in water – do not puncture or open can – and boil about 2 hours. Be sure the water does not boil away. When the boiling is complete, put the unopened can in the refrigerator. Open the can the next day. It makes soft, caramel candy.

Million Dollar Fudge

When sugar rationing ended after World War II, it was a great treat to make candy. Bessie, a wonderful cook and one of God's angels on earth, gave me this recipe.

4 & ½-cups granulated sugar
A pinch of salt
2-tablespoons butter
1, 12-ounce can evaporated milk
1, 12-ounce package semisweet chocolate bits
1, 12-ounce package German sweet chocolate
1-pint marshmallow crème
2-cups pecans or walnuts, chopped

Boil sugar, salt, butter, and milk for 6-minutes. Put remainder of ingredients into a large bowl. Pour boiling sugar syrup over the ingredients in the bowl. Beat until chocolate is melted and pour into pan. Let stand for a few hours before cutting. Store in cookie tin.

Chocolate Cocoa Fudge

The girls in my neighborhood and I made this candy on Sunday afternoons.

3-cups granulated sugar

½-cup cocoa

½-teaspoon salt

1 & ½-cups whole milk

4 & ½-tablespoons butter

1-teaspoon vanilla

Combine sugar, cocoa, and salt. Add milk and bring to a boil, stirring often. Cook until it forms a soft ball in cold water. Remove from heat. Add butter. Cool. Add vanilla and beat until thickened and glossy. Spread in a lightly greased pan.

Cheese Fudge

My sister, Mabel, was given this recipe from a friend in Huntsville, Alabama.

Prepare 2, 9 x 12-inch glass dishes, lightly buttered.

1-pound Velveeta Cheese

1-pound butter

4-packages confectioners sugar (1-pound)

1-cup baking cocoa

1-tablespoon vanilla extract

3-cups chopped nuts

Melt Velveeta Cheese and butter in a saucepan over low heat, stirring frequently. Sift confectioners sugar and cocoa together until mixed well. Combine cheese mixture and cocoa mixture in a large bowl. Mix well. Add vanilla and nuts. Mix well. Spread into 2, lightly buttered, 9 x 12-inch glass dishes. Let stand until firm. This freezes well.

Peanut Butter Fudge
A delicious Christmas gift.
Prepare 8-inch square pan with butter.

¾-cup evaporated milk
¼-cup butter or margarine
2 & ¼-cups sugar
1, 7-ounce jar marshmallow crème
1-teaspoon vanilla
1, 12-ounce package Reese's peanut butter chips
1-cup chopped pecans
¼-cup candied green cherries cut in quarters
Whole green and red cherries and pecan halves, for decoration

Combine evaporated milk, butter, sugar, and marshmallow crème in a heavy 2 & ¾-quart saucepan. Cook over medium heat until mixture begins to boil, stirring constantly. Continue cooking and stirring for 5-minutes. Remove from heat and stir in vanilla. Immediately add peanut butter chips, stirring until they completely melt. Stir in pecan pieces and quartered candied cherries. Pour into prepared pan. Decorate with whole cherries and pecan halves. Cool. Cut into squares.

Potato Candy

¼-cup hot mashed potatoes
1-teaspoon melted butter
1 & ¾-cups confectioners sugar, sifted
1 & ½-cups flaked coconut
Pinch of salt
¼-teaspoon orange rind, grated
½-teaspoon vanilla

Combine potatoes and butter in a medium bowl. Gradually add sugar, beating until thoroughly blended. Add remaining ingredients, mixing well. Drop by teaspoonful onto wax paper. Let stand until firm. Yield: about 2-dozen.

Pecan Peanut Butter Balls

1-pound butter or margarine
2-pounds peanut butter
3-pounds confectioners sugar, sifted
1-cup chopped pecans
2-pounds semi-sweet chocolate

Melt margarine and mix well with peanut butter and sugar. Add pecans to dough-like mixture. Roll dough into balls about 1-inch in size. Set on wax paper. Melt chocolate into double boiler. Using a spoon, dip balls into chocolate, coating each one well. Set on waxed paper and cool. Makes about 200 pieces of candy.

Chocolate Peanut Clusters

Use a 1 & ½-quart saucepan.

1-package chocolate pudding, not instant
1-cup sugar
½-cup evaporated milk
1-tablespoon butter

Mix pudding, sugar, evaporated milk, and butter in saucepan. Cook and stir to a full, all over, boil. Lower heat and keep stirring while mixture boils slowly for 3-minutes. Remove from heat. Stir in 1-cup small, salted peanuts. Beat until candy starts to thicken. Drop from a teaspoon onto waxed paper to form 24-clusters.

Mama's Pineapple Sherbet

When I was a young child, Mama made this summer afternoon treat for me.

1, 8-ounce can crushed pineapple, not drained

1-cup sugar

2-cups buttermilk

1-tablespoon vanilla

2-egg whites

Mix together crushed pineapple, sugar, buttermilk, and vanilla. Place in ice cube tray. After it is partially frozen, remove from freezer. Beat egg whites until stiff peaks form. Fold in egg whites. Return to freezer. Let freeze until it sets firmly.

BEVERAGES

Brandy Ice
A lovely light dessert.

1 & ½-ounces French Brandy
1 ounce White Crème de Cocoa
Vanilla ice cream
Dash nutmeg

Fill blender half-full with soft vanilla ice cream. Add French Brandy White Crème de Cocoa. Blend to semi-liquid. Serve with a dash of nutmeg in a Champagne glass with cookies on the side.

Boonesborough's Favorite Punch

1-pint pineapple juice
1-cup lemon juice
1-pint ice tea
1-quart Ginger Ale
1-quart orange juice
1-pint Bourbon
2-cups sugar
1-pint water

Make syrup to sweeten punch by boiling 2-cups sugar with 1-pint water. Boil about 10-minutes. Cool and add to ingredients above.

Derby Daiquiri

½ ounce fresh lime juice
1-ounce fresh orange juice
1-teaspoon light Rum
1-cup shaved or crushed ice

Combine all ingredients in a blender. Set on medium speed for 20 seconds. Pour into a chilled 8-ounce glass. One serving.

Nacho's Coffee

1-cube sugar

¼-ounce brandy

¼-cup coffee

1-ounce Tequila

    Top with unsweetened whipped cream. One serving.

Christmas Tea Punch
Excellent for an open house party.

2-quarts tea

2, 6-ounce cans frozen limeade

2, 6-ounce cans frozen lemonade

2-cups cranberry juice

2, 28-ounce bottles Ginger Ale

    Pour tea into punch bowl. Add all the juices. Place ice ring or ice cubes into bowl. Add Ginger Ale just before serving.

Percolator Wassail

4-cups apple cider

4-cups cranberry-apple juice

3-tablespoons brown sugar

½-teaspoon whole allspice

1-teaspoon whole cloves

3-cinnamon sticks

¼-teaspoon salt

1-orange with peel cut into wedges

    Pour apple cider and cranberry-apple juice into lower part of a 10 to 12-cup electric coffee maker. In the basket of the coffee maker, place all the remaining ingredients. Cover and let perk.